WHEN THE SIREN SOUNDS

Tom Bourne

Toucan Press

CONTENTS

PREFACE

This book examines fatal mining prosecutions in Australia between 2015 and 2025. It does not attempt to catalogue every fatality. It does not revisit coronial findings in full. It does not assign moral commentary.

It examines how death intersects with statutory architecture.

Mining is chosen deliberately. It is a high-risk industry operating within structured regulatory environments. It has experienced sustained legislative reform during the decade examined, including the introduction and expansion of industrial manslaughter provisions in several jurisdictions.

Public discussion frequently assumes that legislative change necessarily produces criminal conviction. The record of fatal mining prosecutions during this period provides a more measured narrative.

This manuscript focuses on:

Primary duty prosecutions.
Reckless conduct provisions.
Industrial manslaughter frameworks.
Officer due diligence exposure.
Psychosocial risk integration.

The scope is confined to Australia and to the decade 2015–2025 to maintain evidentiary coherence.

The analysis is grounded in:

Court sentencing remarks.
Prosecution summaries.

Regulator releases.
Legislative provisions.
Publicly available technical findings.

Where possible, this manuscript relies on judicial language rather than secondary commentary. The intention is not to reinterpret findings beyond their documented scope.

Throughout the decade examined, mining fatalities were prosecuted primarily within breach frameworks. Industrial manslaughter convictions did not emerge in mining during this period.

This fact alone invites structured analysis.

The absence of conviction does not imply absence of hazard. It invites examination of evidentiary threshold.

Mining operations during this period generally maintained formal safety systems. Fatal incidents often arose from implementation failure rather than total absence of control architecture.

The legal question is not whether risk existed. The legal question is whether documented evidence demonstrated criminal negligence beyond reasonable doubt.

This manuscript approaches that question methodically.

It identifies patterns across hazard domains. It analyses prosecutorial decision-making. It examines sentencing calibration. It models governance exposure. It considers future evidentiary evolution.

It does not advocate. It does not criticise. It records and analyses.

Mining fatalities carry human weight. That weight is not diminished by legal analysis. The purpose of this book is not to revisit personal tragedy. It is to examine how the law responds to it.

The siren signals operational crisis. In court, it signals evidentiary scrutiny.

Between 2015 and 2025, the courtroom siren did not consistently cross the threshold into industrial manslaughter in mining.

Understanding why requires disciplined examination.

This book provides it.

INTRODUCTION

Mining, Law and the Threshold of Criminality

Mining is inherently hazardous. The scale of energy, depth of excavation, mobility of heavy plant and volatility of geological environments create persistent exposure to fatal risk. No decade has eliminated that reality.

Between 2015 and 2025, Australia experienced continued mining fatalities within an evolving legal environment. Industrial manslaughter provisions were introduced or strengthened in multiple jurisdictions. Reckless conduct offences were available. Officer due diligence duties were clarified and emphasised.

Public expectation often assumes that legislative expansion will necessarily produce criminal escalation.

The record of mining fatality prosecutions during this decade presents a more nuanced picture.

This book examines how the law responded.

Scope and Structure

This manuscript is structured deliberately.

Part I examines foundational legal doctrine. It sets out the statutory framework governing primary duties, reckless conduct and industrial manslaughter across key mining jurisdictions.

Part II examines hazard domains central to fatal mining prosecutions during the decade:
Mobile plant interaction.
Ground and strata instability.
Mechanical isolation failure.
Explosion and gas exposure.
Fatigue and psychosocial risk.

Each domain is analysed not merely as an operational hazard but as a prosecutorial pathway. The focus is evidentiary: what was known, what was implemented and what was proven.

Part III examines escalation architecture:
Industrial manslaughter provisions.
Officer due diligence liability.
Sentencing trends.
Comparative jurisdictional approaches.
Prosecutorial decision-making models.

Part IV synthesises systemic patterns and models future exposure.

The book concludes by examining how evidence, rather than legislative symbolism, controls the boundary between breach and criminal negligence.

The Central Question

Throughout this decade, mining fatalities were prosecuted. Fines were imposed. Judicial remarks identified failure of implementation, supervision and escalation.

Industrial manslaughter convictions in mining did not occur.

Why?

The answer is not found in political rhetoric. It is found in evidence.

Criminal law requires proof beyond reasonable doubt of conduct so far below standard that it constitutes criminal negligence or recklessness.

The prosecutions examined in this book demonstrate that:

Hazards were recognised.
Systems were documented.
Controls were partially implemented.
Escalation was imperfect.

They do not consistently demonstrate documented conscious disregard of imminent fatal risk at executive level.

This evidentiary distinction explains the prosecutorial outcomes observed.

Mining as Case Study

Mining is selected as the focus for a reason.

It is technically sophisticated.
It is heavily regulated.
It maintains structured safety governance.
It generates detailed documentation.

If industrial manslaughter were to emerge in a high-risk, well-documented industry, mining would be a likely candidate.

The decade examined provides an empirical baseline.

Evidence Over Assumption

This manuscript does not argue that industrial manslaughter should or should not occur in mining.

It demonstrates that during the period examined, the evidentiary threshold for criminal negligence was not consistently met.

The distinction between:

System failure
and
Criminal indifference

is not rhetorical. It is legal.

Understanding that distinction requires disciplined review of prosecutions, sentencing remarks and statutory interpretation.

A Structured Analytical Approach

Throughout the book, a structured analytical model is applied:

1. Identify documented systems.
2. Assess implementation integrity.
3. Map escalation pathways.
4. Analyse documentation of knowledge.
5. Evaluate officer awareness.
6. Assess causation clarity.
7. Apply statutory threshold.

This model reflects patterns observable across fatal mining prosecutions between 2015 and 2025.

It is not speculative.

It is derived from documented cases.

The Purpose of This Book

This book is not written to provoke.

It is written to clarify.

Fatal mining incidents are tragic events. Legal analysis does not diminish their human impact. It examines how the justice system categorises conduct following such events.

The courtroom siren sounds differently from the operational siren.

It asks:

What was known?
What was decided?
What was done?
What can be proven?

Between 2015 and 2025, those questions produced a consistent outcome in mining prosecutions.

The chapters that follow examine that outcome in detail.

CHAPTER 1

Mining Fatalities in Australia (2015–2025): Statistical, Structural and Enforcement Context

Between 1 January 2015 and 31 March 2025, mining remained one of Australia's highest consequence industries in terms of fatal workplace risk. Safe Work Australia's annual "Work-related Traumatic Injury Fatalities" reports across this period consistently identified mining as recording a fatality rate per 100,000 workers that exceeded the national average.

Absolute numbers varied annually. Some years recorded single-digit fatalities. Other years recorded low double-digit figures. However, rate-based analysis is more meaningful than raw numbers. Mining employs a comparatively smaller workforce than construction, agriculture or transport. A smaller denominator amplifies fatality rate sensitivity. The persistence of elevated rates over time indicates systemic exposure to high energy hazards.

Fatal incidents during the decade examined occurred in underground coal operations, underground metalliferous mines, surface coal mines and quarry operations. Each operational environment involves distinct risk clusters, yet the mechanisms of fatal injury display structural consistency.

Regulator investigation summaries and sentencing remarks across the decade identify recurring fatal mechanisms:

Interaction between pedestrians and heavy mobile plant.
Ground or rib collapse within underground environments.
Failure or degradation of ground support systems.
Entanglement in rotating machinery during maintenance tasks.

Release of stored hydraulic or mechanical energy during isolation failures.

The recurrence of these mechanisms is legally relevant. The reasonably practicable test is anchored in foreseeability. Where hazard categories are repeatedly documented in regulator alerts, coronial recommendations and prior prosecutions, knowledge cannot be characterised as novel.

Mining does not present hidden risks. It presents known high consequence risks that require disciplined control.

Structural Characteristics of Mining Risk

Mining differs from many other industries in three structurally significant ways.

First, the energy profile is high. Heavy mobile plant in surface coal operations may weigh hundreds of tonnes. Underground haul trucks operate within confined declines where visibility is limited and escape routes are constrained. Crushers and conveyors operate under substantial torque and stored mechanical force.

Second, geological variability introduces dynamic instability. Underground coal operations experience stress redistribution and methane accumulation. Metalliferous operations encounter rock mass variability influenced by excavation geometry and blasting sequences.

Third, operational continuity increases exposure duration. Mines operate on rotating shifts. Fatigue management becomes critical. Maintenance windows occur within compressed time frames to maintain production targets.

These characteristics do not lower statutory obligations. They increase the expectation that systematic risk control be robust.

Enforcement Patterns Across the Decade

Regulatory enforcement between 2015 and 2025 displayed measurable stability. Following a fatal incident, regulators typically undertook:

Immediate site preservation.
Securing of plant and equipment involved.
Collection of management plans and risk assessments.
Formal interviews under statutory powers.
Engagement of subject matter experts in geotechnical, mechanical or traffic management disciplines.

Prosecution decisions followed assessment of evidentiary sufficiency under criminal standards.

Across jurisdictions, most fatal mining prosecutions proceeded under primary duty provisions rather than industrial manslaughter statutes.

This pattern reflects evidentiary discipline. Primary duty offences require proof that reasonably practicable measures were available and suitable but not implemented. Industrial manslaughter requires proof of gross or criminal negligence causing death.

The distinction is material.

Coronial and Criminal Interaction

Many fatal mining incidents trigger coronial inquests in addition to regulator investigation. Coronial proceedings examine how a death occurred and may issue recommendations to prevent recurrence.

However, coronial findings operate on a civil standard of proof and are not determinative of criminal liability. Criminal prosecutions require proof beyond reasonable doubt.

In several mining fatalities during the period examined, coronial commentary identified systemic weaknesses. Criminal courts, applying stricter standards, focused on whether specific additional reasonably practicable controls could be established with sufficient certainty.

The interaction between these systems demonstrates an important boundary. The existence of systemic weakness does not automatically equate to criminal negligence.

Rate Versus Reform

The decade between 2015 and 2025 also witnessed significant legislative reform. Western Australia adopted harmonised work health and safety legislation. Queensland strengthened industrial manslaughter provisions. Victoria and the ACT introduced or expanded industrial manslaughter offences.

Despite increased maximum penalties and heightened public focus on accountability, fatal mining prosecutions continued to proceed predominantly under primary duty frameworks.

The absence of industrial manslaughter convictions in mining during this period does not indicate absence of fatality. It indicates the high evidentiary threshold embedded within those provisions.

Fatality as Legal Catalyst

Every fatal mining incident during the decade examined triggered structured legal analysis.

Courts assessed:

What hazards were known.
What controls were implemented.
What additional controls were available.
Whether those controls were suitable in the operational context.
Whether failure to implement those controls amounted to breach.

Where breach was established, penalties reflected the gravity of fatal consequence and the degree of departure from statutory expectation.

Mining fatalities are not analysed in moral terms within criminal courts. They are analysed through statutory criteria.

The remainder of this book applies that framework to recurring hazard domains and specific prosecuted matters between 2015 and 2025.

Fatality Rates in Comparative Perspective

Safe Work Australia reporting during the decade examined consistently demonstrated that the fatality rate in mining remained materially higher than the national all-industry rate. While construction and transport recorded higher absolute numbers, the per capita exposure rate in mining remained comparatively elevated.

This distinction is not rhetorical. Courts assessing reasonably practicable measures consider the likelihood of the hazard occurring. Where an industry's historical data demonstrates repeated fatal mechanisms, the argument that a hazard was unforeseeable weakens considerably.

For example, mobile plant interaction has appeared as a recurrent mechanism in regulator fatality summaries for more than two decades. That continuity informs the "ought reasonably to have known" limb of statutory analysis.

The statistical history of ground control failures similarly demonstrates that rock fall and rib collapse events are not anomalous within underground operations. Regulator publications and mining guidance documents have repeatedly emphasised inspection, scaling and exclusion controls.

In this context, historical fatality data becomes part of the knowledge landscape against which reasonably practicable measures are judged.

Enforcement Evolution Across the Decade

Between 2015 and 2025, regulator enforcement posture in mining did not display abrupt shifts. Instead, it reflected gradual strengthening of evidentiary sophistication.

Earlier matters in the decade tended to focus on physical absence of controls. Later prosecutions more frequently examined adequacy of implementation, verification and supervision.

This evolution is visible in sentencing remarks across jurisdictions. Courts increasingly referenced system verification failures rather than mere absence of documentation.

For example, in mobile plant interaction prosecutions during the latter half of the decade, courts examined whether exclusion zones were physically enforced rather than merely described in management plans.

Similarly, in ground control matters, judicial reasoning increasingly focused on inspection escalation processes and real-time response to precursor instability events.

This progression reflects maturation in enforcement analysis rather than change in statutory duty.

The Boundary Between Tragedy and Criminal Liability

Fatal mining incidents invariably attract public scrutiny. However, criminal liability does not arise from consequence alone.

Courts consistently reiterate that the work health and safety framework is not a regime of strict liability for fatal outcome. The prosecution must prove that reasonably practicable measures were available and suitable and that failure to implement those measures constituted breach.

This boundary is critical in understanding why industrial manslaughter provisions were not applied in mining during the period examined.

Industrial manslaughter requires proof of gross or criminal negligence. That threshold is significantly higher than proof of breach.

Across fatal mining prosecutions during this decade, evidence typically established:

Existing safety management systems.
Documented hazard identification processes.
Recognised though imperfect control frameworks.

Failures often lay in verification, escalation or enforcement rather than in complete absence of safety architecture.

Courts treated these deficiencies as serious. They imposed substantial fines. However, the evidentiary matrix did not generally demonstrate conscious disregard of known and imminent fatal risk.

The distinction between systemic weakness and criminal negligence explains the stability of charging patterns.

Mining Fatalities as Regulatory Catalyst

Fatal incidents often precipitated broader regulatory action beyond prosecution. Regulators issued safety alerts, conducted industry-wide audits and amended guidance material.

These responses underscore that fatal mining incidents function as catalysts for regulatory reinforcement.

However, regulatory learning does not retroactively establish criminal negligence. Courts assess conduct at the time of the incident, based on knowledge and available controls then existing.

This temporal focus is essential. Hindsight improvements in safety practice do not automatically convert earlier conduct into criminal negligence.

Structural Stability in Charging Decisions

Between 2015 and 2025, fatal mining prosecutions predominantly proceeded under primary duty frameworks rather than Category 1 recklessness or industrial manslaughter provisions.

This pattern suggests that regulators assessed evidence against the higher thresholds and concluded that proof of recklessness or gross negligence was not available to the required criminal standard.

The absence of industrial manslaughter convictions in mining during this period therefore reflects evidentiary calibration rather than reluctance to prosecute.

As legislative reform expanded maximum penalties and introduced imprisonment exposure for officers, mining prosecutions nonetheless remained anchored in demonstrable breach rather than criminal indifference.

Conclusion

The decade between 2015 and 2025 presents a consistent legal picture.

Mining remained a high consequence industry.
Fatal incidents occurred within known hazard domains.
Regulators investigated systematically.
Courts applied statutory tests with discipline.
Industrial manslaughter provisions were not invoked to conviction in the mining sector.

Understanding this stability requires careful attention to statutory thresholds, evidentiary burden and the distinction between breach and gross negligence.

The chapters that follow examine specific hazard domains and prosecuted matters within that framework.

Chapter References

Safe Work Australia (2015–2024) *Work-related Traumatic Injury Fatalities Reports.* Canberra: Safe Work Australia.

Department of Mines, Industry Regulation and Safety (DMIRS) (2015–2025) *Prosecution Media Releases and Annual Reports.* Government of Western Australia.

Resources Safety and Health Queensland (RSHQ) (2015–2025) *Prosecution Summaries and Annual Safety Performance Reports.* Queensland Government.

Work Health and Safety Act 2011 (Qld).

Work Health and Safety Act 2020 (WA).

Resources Safety and Health Act 2020 (Qld).

CHAPTER 2

Methodology, Scope and Evidentiary Parameters

1. Purpose of the Study

This book examines mining fatality prosecutions in Western Australia and Queensland between 1 January 2015 and 31 December 2025. It does not attempt to catalogue every mining incident during that period. Nor does it seek to revisit the technical engineering dimensions of each event in forensic detail. Its focus is narrower and more specific: to analyse how statutory duties were interpreted, charged and adjudicated in fatal mining matters, and to identify the evidentiary boundary between regulatory breach and criminal negligence.

The central research question is not whether fatalities occurred. It is why industrial manslaughter convictions did not emerge within the mining sector during the period examined, despite the existence of relevant statutory provisions.

To answer that question requires disciplined scope and transparent method.

2. Jurisdictional Focus

The analysis concentrates on Western Australia and Queensland for several reasons.

First, both jurisdictions have large-scale mining operations across coal, metalliferous and underground environments. They represent the most significant mining regulatory landscapes in Australia.

Second, Queensland introduced industrial manslaughter provisions into the Work Health and Safety Act 2011 in 2017. Western Australia introduced comparable provisions through the Work Health and Safety Act 2020. These reforms create a relevant legislative window within the timeframe examined.

Third, both jurisdictions publish prosecution summaries, media releases, annual reports and, in some cases, sentencing remarks that allow structured legal analysis.

New South Wales and other jurisdictions are referenced comparatively where necessary, but the evidentiary emphasis remains on WA and QLD.

---

3. Temporal Scope

The period 2015–2025 was selected deliberately.

It captures:

- The pre-industrial manslaughter enforcement environment
- The introduction of industrial manslaughter provisions
- The maturation of harmonised officer due diligence obligations
- A full decade of regulator charging behaviour

A shorter timeframe would risk anecdotal conclusions. A longer timeframe would dilute legislative comparability.

This decade allows examination of enforcement patterns after reform, rather than speculation before it.

---

4. Source Material

The analysis draws exclusively from publicly verifiable materials, including:

- Work Health and Safety legislation in WA and QLD
- Mining-specific safety legislation and regulations

- Explanatory memoranda and parliamentary debates
- Regulator prosecution summaries
- Annual performance and enforcement reports
- Publicly available sentencing remarks
- Safe Work Australia statistical publications
- Official safety alerts and guidance material

No reliance is placed on confidential corporate data, internal documents, or unpublished regulator briefs.

Where sentencing remarks are not publicly available in full, regulator summaries are used cautiously and without embellishment.

This constraint shapes the level of detail presented in micro-case reconstructions.

---

5. Micro-Case Reconstruction Method

Several chapters use "micro-case reconstruction" rather than named case analysis.

This is intentional.

Public prosecution summaries often describe:

- The mechanism of incident
- The duty breached
- The penalty imposed

They rarely provide complete evidentiary transcripts. Reproducing partial factual accounts as though they were complete judicial records risks distortion.

Accordingly, this book:

- Avoids inventing case names
- Avoids attributing facts not contained in public records
- Synthesises patterns drawn from multiple prosecutions
- Uses reconstructed factual scenarios that reflect documented enforcement themes

These reconstructions are not fictional. They are pattern-based composites grounded in published regulator descriptions. Their purpose is analytical clarity, not narrative drama.

This approach prevents the inflation of isolated facts into general conclusions.

---

6. Analytical Framework

The analysis operates through five structured lenses:

1. Hazard Domain Analysis
   Examining recurrent fatal categories including mobile plant, ground control, mechanical isolation and gas management.
2. Hierarchy of Control Application
   Evaluating whether engineering controls were reasonably available and whether administrative reliance attracted judicial criticism.
3. Officer Due Diligence Threshold
   Assessing the evidentiary burden required to establish personal liability.
4. Charging Calibration
   Comparing Category 1, 2 and 3 offences with industrial manslaughter provisions.
5. Evidentiary Boundary Mapping
   Identifying what additional facts would likely have been required to elevate matters to criminal negligence.

This layered framework ensures that the book does not merely describe prosecutions, but evaluates their legal architecture.

---

7. Limitations

Several limitations must be acknowledged.

First, regulator summaries do not disclose full evidentiary briefs. Charging decisions may have been influenced by material not publicly released.

Second, absence of industrial manslaughter convictions does not equate to absence of prosecutorial consideration.

Third, statistical fatality data reflects reported incidents and may not capture all contributing enforcement interactions.

Fourth, this study does not assess civil compensation claims, coronial recommendations, or union-initiated proceedings except where directly relevant to criminal enforcement.

Transparency regarding these limitations strengthens rather than weakens the conclusions drawn.

---

8. Defining "Evidentiary Boundary"

The term "evidentiary boundary" is used repeatedly throughout this book. It refers to the practical threshold at which:

• A breach of statutory duty
becomes
• Criminal negligence of a gross character

In industrial manslaughter provisions, this boundary requires proof of conduct representing a gross departure from the standard of care a reasonable person would exercise in the circumstances.

The word "gross" is not rhetorical. It is legal.

Understanding why prosecutions did not cross that threshold in mining during the decade examined requires disciplined attention to what courts require, not what public discourse demands.

---

9. Data Versus Narrative

Mining fatalities attract intense public reaction. Commentary frequently frames such events in moral or emotive terms.

This book adopts a different approach.

It separates:

• Moral outrage from
• Prosecutable evidence

The absence of an industrial manslaughter conviction does not imply regulatory indifference. It may reflect evidentiary insufficiency.

The purpose of this study is not to defend corporate actors nor to criticise regulators. It is to examine the structure of enforcement and identify patterns that emerge from documented decisions.

---

10. Why This Method Matters

Without disciplined scope and evidentiary transparency, analysis risks becoming speculative.

Speculation is easy in fatality discourse.

Precision is harder.

By confining analysis to verifiable sources, acknowledging limitations, and clearly distinguishing reconstruction from adjudicated fact, this study preserves credibility while still engaging critically with enforcement outcomes.

The chapters that follow move hazard domain by hazard domain, then ascend to officer liability, prosecutorial calibration and legislative philosophy.

The objective is not simply to describe what occurred.

It is to determine what did not occur, and why.

Chapter References

Work Health and Safety Act 2011 (Qld).

Work Health and Safety Act 2020 (WA).

Resources Safety and Health Act 2020 (Qld).

Criminal Code Act 1899 (Qld).

R v Lavender (2005) 222 CLR 67.

Queensland Parliament (2017) *Explanatory Notes – Work Health and Safety and Other Legislation Amendment Bill 2017*.

Parliament of Western Australia (2019) *Second Reading Speech – Work Health and Safety Bill 2019.*

Director of Public Prosecutions (Queensland) *Guidelines for Prosecutors*

Office of the Director of Public Prosecutions (WA) *Prosecution Policy and Guidelines*

CHAPTER 3

Mobile Plant Interaction Fatalities: Engineering Controls, System Failure and Evidentiary Limits

Mobile plant interaction remains one of the most persistent fatal hazard domains within Australian mining. Between 2015 and 2025, regulator reports across Western Australia and Queensland repeatedly recorded fatalities arising from interaction between heavy vehicles and light vehicles, and between mobile plant and workers on foot.

The persistence of this hazard category is legally significant. Mobile plant interaction is neither rare nor novel. It is well understood. Courts therefore approach prosecutions from a position in which foreseeability is rarely contested. The statutory question becomes whether, so far as reasonably practicable, additional engineering or supervisory controls were available and not implemented.

Structural Risk Profile

Mining operations depend on high-energy mobile equipment. Underground haul trucks operate in confined declines and cross-cut intersections. Surface coal mines rely on large rear-dump trucks operating on haul roads in proximity to service vehicles and personnel.

The risk environment includes:

- Restricted line-of-sight visibility
- Blind spots inherent in heavy equipment design
- Complex underground geometry

- Fatigue exposure in extended roster patterns
- Reliance on radio communication protocols
- Variable braking conditions due to ground and weather

The potential consequence of uncontrolled interaction is fatal injury.

Western Australia: Karlawinda Fatal Collision

In October 2022, a worker was fatally injured at the Karlawinda gold mine in Western Australia following a collision involving a dump truck and a light vehicle. In October 2024, WorkSafe WA commenced prosecutions under the Work Health and Safety Act 2020 (WA) against both the mining contractor and the principal operator (WorkSafe WA 2024).

The prosecution illustrates several recurrent themes in mobile plant fatality enforcement:

- Traffic management system adequacy
- Segregation of heavy and light vehicles
- Communication protocol enforcement
- Contractor and principal overlapping duties
- Supervision and verification mechanisms

The regulator did not allege industrial manslaughter. Charges were laid under primary duty provisions. This reflects prosecutorial calibration aligned with available evidence.

The legal issue was not whether mobile plant interaction risk was known. It was whether reasonably practicable additional controls were available and not implemented.

Western Australia: Pilbara Multi-Contractor Liability

In 2025, multiple entities were fined a combined $770,000 following the death of a truck driver at a Pilbara mine site (WorkSafe WA 2025). The case is significant for its treatment of overlapping duties in contractor environments.

The court examined:

- Allocation of traffic management responsibility
- Interface between principal and subcontractor systems
- Verification of exclusion zones
- Enforcement of vehicle separation

The existence of documented procedures did not prevent conviction. Judicial reasoning focused on implementation failure rather than policy absence.

Engineering Controls and the Hierarchy Principle

Across jurisdictions, courts apply the hierarchy of control in mobile plant cases.

Engineering controls are preferred over administrative reliance.

Engineering controls in mobile plant environments may include:

- Physical separation of pedestrian and vehicle routes
- Dedicated light vehicle lanes
- One-way traffic systems
- Proximity detection or collision avoidance technology
- Intersection redesign to eliminate blind geometry

Administrative controls include:

- Traffic management plans
- Radio call-up protocols
- Signage and speed limits
- Training and induction

Judicial reasoning during the decade examined consistently emphasised that administrative instruction cannot substitute for reasonably available engineering separation where fatal risk is foreseeable.

The Role of Near Miss Data

Mining operations routinely record near miss events. In mobile plant prosecutions, near miss records are legally significant.

They establish knowledge.

Where internal reporting demonstrates repeated vehicle interaction warnings, the prosecution may rely upon those records to show that risk was not theoretical.

However, near miss data alone does not establish recklessness. To escalate a matter to Category 1 or industrial manslaughter, evidence would need to show:

- Escalating interaction frequency
- Clear engineering solutions identified
- Deliberate failure to act despite imminent fatal probability

The matters prosecuted during 2015–2025 did not meet that threshold.

Proximity Detection Technology and Reasonably Practicable Analysis

Collision avoidance and proximity detection systems became increasingly available during the latter half of the decade.

The reasonably practicable analysis in relation to such technology requires examination of:

- Suitability for underground or surface environment
- Integration with fleet systems
- Reliability in operational conditions
- Cost relative to risk

Courts require evidence that technology was available, suitable and not grossly disproportionate in cost before concluding that failure to implement constituted breach.

In the examined matters, convictions were secured without establishing that non-installation of advanced technology alone amounted to gross negligence.

Fatigue and Human Factors

Mobile plant operation intersects with fatigue management. Extended shifts and night operations affect reaction time.

In prosecutions reviewed during the period, fatigue was occasionally raised in sentencing submissions. However, regulators typically framed breach around physical control failures rather than fatigue policy alone.

This reflects evidentiary practicality. Proving absence of engineering separation is more direct than proving fatigue causation beyond reasonable doubt.

The Industrial Manslaughter Boundary

No industrial manslaughter conviction arose in an Australian mining mobile plant fatality between 2015 and 2025.

To elevate a mobile plant fatality to industrial manslaughter, prosecutors would likely require evidence of:

- Documented warnings of imminent fatal interaction
- Rejection of identified engineering solutions without risk justification
- Senior officer awareness of escalating fatal probability
- Conscious continuation of operations despite that knowledge

The prosecuted matters of this decade demonstrated serious system deficiencies.

They did not demonstrate criminal indifference at the gross negligence threshold.

Conclusion

Mobile plant interaction remains a dominant fatal hazard domain in Australian mining.

Between 2015 and 2025, prosecutions reinforced that:

- Foreseeability is rarely disputed
- Engineering controls carry primacy
- Documentation alone does not discharge duty
- Overlapping contractor duties attract independent scrutiny
- The boundary between breach and criminal negligence remains

high

Convictions proceeded under primary duty provisions.

Industrial manslaughter remained legally untested in this domain during the period examined.

Chapter References

Department of Mines, Industry Regulation and Safety (DMIRS) (2015–2025) *Prosecution media releases and enforcement summaries.* Government of Western Australia. Available at: https://www.dmirs.wa.gov.au

Resources Safety and Health Queensland (RSHQ) (2015–2025) *Prosecution summaries and safety alerts – mobile plant and vehicle interaction.* Queensland Government. Available at: https://www.rshq.qld.gov.au

Safe Work Australia (2023) *Work-related traumatic injury fatalities, Australia.* Canberra: Safe Work Australia.

Work Health and Safety Act 2011 (Qld).

Work Health and Safety Act 2020 (WA).

R v Lavender (2005) 222 CLR 67.

Mining and Quarrying Safety and Health Act 1999 (Qld).

Mines Safety and Inspection Act 1994 (WA) (as in force during relevant period).

CHAPTER 4

Mobile Plant Interaction and Vehicle Collision: Proximity, Control and Foreseeability

Mobile plant interaction remains one of the most persistent fatal risk domains in Australian mining. Light vehicles, haul trucks, loaders and ancillary equipment operate in shared spaces where visibility, communication and separation systems are critical.

Between 2015 and 2025, prosecutions in Western Australia demonstrate how regulators examine traffic management, segregation controls and contractor interface when fatal collisions occur.

Karlawinda Mine Fatal Collision (M-02)

In October 2022, a fatal collision occurred at the Karlawinda mine site involving a dump truck and a light vehicle. In October 2024, WorkSafe WA commenced prosecutions under the Work Health and Safety Act 2020 (WA) against both the mining contractor and the site operator (WorkSafe WA 2024).

The prosecutions were significant as among the first fatality matters commenced under the new WHS Act framework in Western Australia.

While the matter was ongoing at the time of announcement, the regulator's position reflects the evidentiary focus typical of mobile plant fatalities:

- Traffic management plan adequacy
- Physical segregation controls
- Right-of-way systems

- Communication protocols
- Supervision and enforcement
- Contractor and principal duty allocation

The central statutory question is whether, so far as reasonably practicable, the duty holder ensured the health and safety of workers exposed to mobile plant interaction risk.

The fact that multiple entities were charged underscores a structural feature of contemporary mining enforcement: overlapping duties are examined independently.

Pilbara Earthworks Fatality – Multi-Contractor Interface (M-03)

In 2025, multiple companies were fined a combined $770,000 in relation to the death of a truck driver at a Pilbara mine site (WorkSafe WA 2025).

The prosecution illustrates how regulators analyse contractor interface in plant-related fatalities. Rather than isolating fault to a single entity, enforcement examined:

- Role clarity between contractor and principal
- Allocation of traffic management responsibility
- Implementation of safe work method statements
- Verification of exclusion zones

Sentencing emphasised failure of implementation rather than absence of documented systems.
The existence of a traffic management plan did not preclude conviction. What mattered was whether the controls operated effectively in the field.

Foreseeability and Control

Mobile plant interaction hazards are not novel risks. Visibility limitations, blind spots, communication breakdowns and speed differentials are well understood in mining environments.

Courts consistently assess whether reasonably practicable controls included:

- Engineered separation
- Physical barriers
- Technology-assisted proximity detection
- Clear procedural enforcement

The absence of industrial manslaughter charges in these matters does not reflect low seriousness. It reflects prosecutorial calibration aligned with available evidence.

To escalate to criminal negligence of the industrial manslaughter type, evidence would likely need to demonstrate conscious disregard of repeated collision warnings or systemic abandonment of segregation controls.

Such matrices were not present in the prosecuted matters of this decade.

Conclusion

Mobile plant fatalities during 2015–2025 reinforced that:

- Overlapping duties are examined independently
- Contractor interface increases evidentiary complexity
- Documentation alone does not discharge statutory obligation
- Implementation failure remains the dominant prosecutorial theme

Chapter References

Resources Safety and Health Queensland (RSHQ) (2015–2025) *Ground control safety alerts and prosecution summaries*. Queensland Government.

Department of Mines, Industry Regulation and Safety (DMIRS) (2015–2025) *Ground stability and strata control enforcement actions*. Government of Western Australia.

Safe Work Australia (2023) *Work-related traumatic injury fatalities, Australia*.

Coal Mining Safety and Health Regulation 2017 (Qld).

Mining and Quarrying Safety and Health Act 1999 (Qld).

Work Health and Safety Act 2020 (WA).

R v Lavender (2005) 222 CLR 67.

CHAPTER 5

Ground Control and Strata Failure: Engineering Knowledge and Implementation Breakdown

Ground instability in underground mining presents a foreseeable and well-characterised hazard. Modern strata management systems incorporate geotechnical modelling, monitoring instrumentation and engineered support systems.

Between 2015 and 2025, prosecutions arising from ground control failures reflect judicial focus on implementation integrity rather than absence of knowledge.

Hamlet Underground Mine – Fatal Rock Fall (M-01)

In 2022, a fatal rock fall occurred during underground raisebore work at the Hamlet gold mine in Western Australia. In September 2025, RUC Mining Contractors Pty Ltd was fined $540,000 following conviction under the Work Health and Safety Act 2020 (WA) (WorkSafe WA 2025).

The prosecution examined:

- Ground support installation
- Risk assessment prior to re-entry
- Supervision of underground work
- Verification of geotechnical controls

The court's reasoning reinforced a consistent theme: the presence of engineering systems does not discharge duty where field verification is deficient.

There was no industrial manslaughter charge. The evidentiary threshold required for gross criminal negligence was not established.

Carborough Downs Coal Mine – Strata Failure and Serious Harm (M-05)

In Queensland, the Carborough Downs prosecution resulted in a $720,000 fine following a fatality and serious injury arising from strata failure in 2019 (Office of the Work Health and Safety Prosecutor 2024).

The matter demonstrates how Queensland enforcement approaches underground hazards. The prosecution centred on:

- Compliance with ground support plans
- Hazard identification processes
- Supervisory enforcement
- Risk assessment adequacy

Sentencing remarks emphasised implementation failure.

The statutory framework required the operator to ensure safety so far as reasonably practicable. The court found that threshold unmet.

Engineering Plans and Re-Entry Risk

Ground control prosecutions frequently involve re-entry into unsupported headings or areas where stress redistribution is anticipated.

Where documented engineering advice identifies instability risk, evidentiary focus shifts to:

- Whether re-entry was authorised appropriately
- Whether inspection protocols were followed
- Whether support installation was verified

To escalate such failures to industrial manslaughter would require evidence that management knowingly permitted exposure to imminent collapse risk.

Such evidence did not arise in the examined matters.

Conclusion

Ground control prosecutions during 2015–2025 demonstrate:

- Courts defer to engineering expertise but scrutinise implementation
- Documentation without verification does not discharge duty
- Criminal thresholds remain high

Chapter References

Resources Safety and Health Queensland (RSHQ) (2015–2025) *Isolation failures and plant maintenance prosecution summaries.* Queensland Government.

Department of Mines, Industry Regulation and Safety (DMIRS) (2015–2025) *Prosecution media releases – maintenance and isolation incidents.* Government of Western Australia.

Safe Work Australia (2023) *Work-related traumatic injury fatalities, Australia.*

Work Health and Safety Act 2011 (Qld).

Work Health and Safety Act 2020 (WA).

Managing Risks of Plant in the Workplace – Code of Practice (Safe Work Australia).

R v Lavender (2005) 222 CLR 67.

CHAPTER 6

Explosions, Gas Management and Ventilation Failure: Catastrophic Risk and Prosecutorial Restraint

Few hazards in mining carry the same catastrophic potential as uncontrolled gas accumulation and ignition. Explosions in underground coal operations have historically resulted in multiple fatalities and widespread destruction. While the period between 2015 and 2025 did not see a mass-fatality explosion in Australian mining comparable to earlier historical events, enforcement activity during this decade demonstrates how regulators analyse gas management, ventilation systems and escalation obligations within contemporary statutory frameworks.

This chapter examines gas exceedance investigations and related prosecutions during the period examined and situates them within the modern evidentiary threshold for criminal liability.

Historical Context and Contemporary Foreseeability

Methane accumulation in underground coal mines is a known hazard. Legislative reform across Australian jurisdictions strengthened ventilation standards, gas monitoring systems and trigger action response plans in response to earlier catastrophic events.

In modern prosecutions, foreseeability of methane ignition risk is rarely disputed. The issue before courts is not whether gas can accumulate. It is whether monitoring systems were maintained, interpreted and acted upon so far as reasonably practicable.

Gas Monitoring and Trigger Action Response Plans

Underground coal operations rely on integrated atmospheric monitoring systems. These include:

- Fixed methane sensors
- Portable gas detectors
- Alarm set-points linked to withdrawal thresholds
- Trigger action response plans (TARPs)

TARPs establish concentration thresholds requiring suspension of activity and withdrawal of personnel. These are not advisory mechanisms. They form part of the operational control architecture against which statutory compliance is assessed.

The NSW Resources Regulator's causal investigation into a significant gas exceedance event at Metropolitan Colliery illustrates this point (NSW Resources Regulator 2021). Elevated methane levels prompted withdrawal of workers; however, the investigation identified deficiencies in system reliability, escalation protocols and communication processes.

Although that event did not result in a fatal prosecution, the investigative analysis demonstrates how regulators examine:

- Calibration and maintenance of gas sensors
- Alarm functionality
- Decision-making timing
- Ventilation adjustment implementation
- Documentation of exceedance management

The legal threshold is implementation integrity, not documentation existence.

Monitoring Integrity and Maintenance Failures

Where monitoring equipment is not calibrated or maintained according to schedule, its protective function is compromised.

While not a methane matter, the prosecution of Orbit Drilling Pty Ltd in Western Australia following a fatal incident involving hydraulic power demonstrates how courts analyse system integrity failures (WorkSafe WA 2021). The court examined whether the employer ensured equipment was used and maintained safely. The existence of procedures did not prevent conviction where field controls failed.

The evidentiary logic is consistent across hazard domains. For methane monitoring:

- A documented maintenance schedule is insufficient if servicing is delayed.
- Alarm thresholds must be verifiable and enforced.
- Supervisory oversight must be demonstrable.

Where monitoring systems are demonstrably unreliable and work continues in reliance upon them, exposure escalates.

Strata Collapse and Gas Risk Interaction

The Carborough Downs prosecution in Queensland, resulting in a $720,000 fine, concerned fatal and serious injuries arising from strata failure (Office of the Work Health and Safety Prosecutor 2024). While not a methane ignition case, it reinforces the broader prosecutorial approach in underground coal operations: implementation failure rather than absence of policy is central.

Courts examine whether management systems were actively verified in the field.

That approach would apply equally in a methane ignition prosecution.

Escalation, Production and Evidentiary Threshold

Prosecutors in the period examined exercised restraint in selecting charge categories in explosion-related contexts.

The absence of industrial manslaughter convictions in explosion-related mining matters between 2015 and 2025 does not indicate regulatory reluctance. It reflects adherence to criminal standards of proof.

To elevate methane exceedance conduct to industrial manslaughter would likely require:

- Repeated high-level exceedances
- Documented engineering advice recommending cessation
- Evidence of conscious continuation of work
- Officer awareness of imminent ignition probability

Such evidentiary matrices were not present in the matters examined during this decade.

Officer Due Diligence in Gas Management

Officers must exercise due diligence by ensuring:

- Adequate ventilation engineering expertise
- Monitoring infrastructure maintenance
- Escalation compliance auditing
- Review of exceedance reports

Between 2015 and 2025, officer prosecutions in explosion-related mining matters were rare. This reflects the difficulty of proving knowledge and conscious disregard, not absence of exposure.

Where corporations demonstrated structured oversight and monitoring systems, officer liability was not established.

Conclusion

Explosion, gas and ventilation failures represent high-consequence hazard domains within mining.

During 2015–2025, enforcement activity reinforced:

- Strict adherence to trigger action response plans
- Maintenance and calibration of monitoring systems
- Immediate withdrawal at defined thresholds
- Executive oversight of ventilation integrity

Chapter References

Resources Safety and Health Queensland (RSHQ) (2015–2025) *Coal mining gas and ventilation safety alerts and prosecution summaries*. Queensland Government.

Department of Mines, Industry Regulation and Safety (DMIRS) (2015–2025) *Underground ventilation and atmospheric monitoring enforcement actions*. Government of Western Australia.

Coal Mining Safety and Health Act 1999 (Qld).

Coal Mining Safety and Health Regulation 2017 (Qld).

Work Health and Safety Act 2020 (WA).

Safe Work Australia (2023) *Work-related traumatic injury fatalities, Australia*.

R v Lavender (2005) 222 CLR 67.

Queensland Parliament (2017) *Explanatory Notes – Work Health and Safety and Other Legislation Amendment Bill 2017*.

CHAPTER 7

Evidentiary Threshold Models: When Does Breach Become Criminal?

Chapters 3 through 6 examined prosecuted fatalities in mobile plant interaction, ground control failure and gas management. Those matters resulted in convictions under primary duty provisions. None resulted in industrial manslaughter convictions within the mining sector during the period examined.

This chapter does not introduce new cases. Instead, it constructs analytical threshold models based on patterns observed in actual prosecutions. The purpose is not speculative prediction. It is evidentiary clarification.

What factual matrix would be required to convert serious breach into criminal negligence?

Model 1: Mobile Plant Escalation Threshold

The prosecutions examined in Western Australia demonstrated that courts focus on implementation failure. Traffic management systems existed. Engineering controls were available in some form. Enforcement was imperfect.

To elevate a mobile plant fatality to industrial manslaughter, the evidentiary matrix would likely require the following elements to converge:

Repeated documented near miss events demonstrating escalating interaction frequency.

Internal safety reports identifying a specific intersection, decline section or haul route as presenting imminent fatal risk.

Engineering redesign options formally proposed and rejected without risk justification.

Senior officer-level awareness of escalating collision probability.

Continued operation in the identified configuration without interim mitigation.

The key element is knowledge combined with conscious inaction. Not general awareness of mobile plant risk. Not imperfect enforcement. But evidence that decision-makers understood the immediacy of fatal risk and chose to continue operations without mitigation.

The prosecuted matters reviewed in Chapters 3 and 4 did not demonstrate that level of evidentiary clarity.

Model 2: Ground Control and Re-Entry Threshold

Ground control prosecutions demonstrated implementation breakdown rather than abandonment of engineering systems.

To cross the criminal threshold in a strata failure scenario, the following factual structure would likely be required:

Geotechnical assessment identifying a defined instability zone.

Explicit engineering recommendation prohibiting re-entry pending support installation.

Management authorisation of re-entry contrary to that advice.

Documented awareness of collapse probability exceeding accepted design parameters.

Failure to implement interim exclusion controls.

The distinction is between engineering error and conscious override of engineering advice.

The Hamlet and Carborough Downs matters involved failures of implementation and supervision. They did not involve proven executive disregard of imminent collapse warnings.

Model 3: Gas Management and Ventilation Escalation

Gas exceedance prosecutions during the decade focused on monitoring and escalation compliance.

To elevate a methane-related fatality to industrial manslaughter, prosecutors would likely require:

Repeated exceedances above statutory trigger levels.

Internal records demonstrating sustained ventilation instability.

Engineering advice recommending withdrawal.

Documented management direction to continue production despite exceedances.

Evidence that decision-makers understood ignition probability and continued regardless.

Absent those elements, courts characterise failures as serious breach rather than gross negligence.

The Metropolitan Colliery investigation illustrates regulatory scrutiny of escalation protocols. It does not demonstrate criminal indifference.

The Role of Officer Knowledge

Industrial manslaughter frameworks require examination of officer-level knowledge and conduct.

Due diligence obligations require officers to:

Acquire knowledge of hazards.

Understand operational risks.

Ensure appropriate resources and processes.

Verify implementation.

Criminal liability arises not from imperfect systems, but from failure to exercise due diligence where fatal risk is foreseeable and escalating.

Between 2015 and 2025, no mining fatality prosecution established that officers knowingly disregarded an imminent fatal hazard in a manner satisfying the criminal threshold.

This is an evidentiary observation, not a policy conclusion.

Prosecutorial Calibration

The absence of industrial manslaughter convictions in mining during this period does not indicate regulatory reluctance.

It reflects prosecutorial calibration aligned with available proof.

Primary duty breaches are easier to establish because they require demonstration of failure to ensure safety so far as reasonably practicable.

Industrial manslaughter requires proof beyond reasonable doubt of gross negligence or reckless indifference.

The distinction is structural.

The prosecutions examined in earlier chapters did not present matrices that crossed that boundary.

Conclusion

The purpose of this chapter is not to argue that mining fatalities are insufficiently serious to warrant criminal sanction.

It is to identify the evidentiary architecture required to convert breach into criminal negligence.

Based on enforcement patterns between 2015 and 2025:

Mobile plant fatalities demonstrated implementation failure.

Ground control fatalities demonstrated supervision breakdown.

Gas-related matters demonstrated escalation deficiencies.

None demonstrated conscious executive disregard of imminent

fatal probability.

The statutory boundary remains evidentiary.

It is not rhetorical.

Chapter References

Office of the Work Health and Safety Prosecutor (Queensland) (2024) Carborough Downs Coal Management Pty Ltd fined $720,000 following fatal underground incident. Queensland Government.

NSW Resources Regulator (2021) Investigation Report: Methane exceedance event, Metropolitan Colliery. NSW Department of Regional NSW.

WorkSafe Western Australia (2024) Prosecution commenced – Karlawinda Mine fatal collision. Government of Western Australia.

WorkSafe Western Australia (2025) Multiple companies fined following fatal truck incident at Pilbara mine site. Government of Western Australia.

WorkSafe Western Australia (2025) RUC Mining Contractors Pty Ltd fined $540,000 following underground fatality at Hamlet mine. Government of Western Australia.

Work Health and Safety Act 2020 (WA).

Work Health and Safety Act 2011 (Qld).

Work Health and Safety Act 2011 (NSW).

CHAPTER 8

Officer Liability in Mining: Due Diligence, Prosecution Patterns and Evidentiary Limits

The harmonised work health and safety framework imposed a direct statutory duty on officers to exercise due diligence to ensure that the person conducting a business or undertaking complies with its duties.

This marked a structural shift in accountability. Liability was no longer confined to the corporate entity. However, due diligence is not strict liability. It requires proof of failure to exercise active oversight.

Between 2015 and 2025, mining fatalities in Western Australia and Queensland resulted in multiple corporate prosecutions. Officer prosecutions were comparatively rare. No industrial manslaughter conviction was secured against a mining officer in Australia during this period.

Understanding that pattern requires examination of statutory architecture and evidentiary threshold.

Statutory Framework

Section 27 of the Work Health and Safety Act 2020 (WA) imposes a duty on officers to exercise due diligence to ensure that the PCBU complies with its obligations.

Due diligence includes taking reasonable steps to:

- Acquire and keep up-to-date knowledge of work health and safety matters

- Understand the nature of operations and associated hazards
- Ensure appropriate resources and processes are provided
- Ensure processes for receiving and considering hazard information exist
- Verify that resources and processes are implemented

Equivalent provisions exist under the Work Health and Safety Act 2011 (Qld) and (NSW).

The duty is proactive. It is not discharged by delegation alone. However, prosecution must prove beyond reasonable doubt that the officer failed to exercise due diligence.

Operational error alone is insufficient.

Mining Prosecution Patterns 2015–2025

Mining prosecutions during this decade primarily targeted corporate entities under primary duty provisions following fatalities in hazard domains including:

- Mobile plant interaction
- Ground and strata failure
- Mechanical isolation
- Gas management

Examples include:

- RUC Mining Contractors Pty Ltd (WA) – Hamlet underground fatality (2025)
- Carborough Downs Coal Management Pty Ltd (Qld) – underground fatality (2024)
- Karlawinda fatal collision prosecution (WA) (2024 commencement)

In these matters, prosecutions focused on system implementation failures rather than executive-level abandonment of safety governance.

Officer charges were not laid in those cases.

This reflects evidentiary limits rather than legislative constraint.

The Knowledge Threshold

Officer liability turns on knowledge and response.

Courts assess whether the officer:

- Knew or ought reasonably to have known of the risk
- Had access to information indicating systemic deficiency
- Failed to respond to that information

In mining prosecutions reviewed during 2015–2025, evidence generally demonstrated that:

- Board-level safety reporting structures existed
- Audit mechanisms were in place
- Safety committees operated
- Risk registers were maintained

Failures occurred at implementation level rather than through demonstrated executive indifference.

That distinction materially constrained officer prosecution.

Verification Versus Delegation

Judicial interpretation of due diligence consistently distinguishes between ensuring systems exist and verifying their effectiveness.

Officers are not expected to supervise day-to-day operations directly. They are required to ensure governance mechanisms capable of detecting failure.

Where structured reporting, audit and resource allocation systems are demonstrable, prosecution must establish that those systems were illusory or knowingly disregarded.

In the mining matters examined during this decade, that evidentiary threshold was not met.

Comparative Non-Mining Officer Convictions

The absence of mining officer convictions is more clearly understood when contrasted with non-mining industrial manslaughter prosecutions.

In Queensland, the first industrial manslaughter conviction under the WHS Act 2011 (Qld) occurred in 2020 against Brisbane Auto Recycling Pty Ltd and its director following the death of a worker crushed by a forklift (R v Jeffrey Owen; Brisbane Auto Recycling Pty Ltd [2020] QDC 113).

The director was sentenced to imprisonment. The court found prolonged and documented disregard of safety requirements and explicit awareness of fatal risk.

The evidentiary matrix included:

- Repeated regulator engagement
- Prior warnings
- Known unsafe practices
- Absence of meaningful corrective action

The degree of indifference established in that case differs materially from the mining prosecutions reviewed during 2015–2025.

The comparison illustrates the level of proof required for criminal negligence findings.

Industrial Manslaughter and Officers

In Western Australia, industrial manslaughter provisions are contained in sections 30A and 30B of the Work Health and Safety Act 2020 (WA).

In Queensland, industrial manslaughter provisions are contained in section 34C of the Work Health and Safety Act 2011 (Qld).

Both require proof of conduct amounting to criminal negligence.

Criminal negligence requires a gross departure from the standard of care that a reasonable person would exercise in the circumstances.

Between 2015 and 2025, although mining fatalities occurred, no prosecution established that an officer's conduct amounted to such gross departure.

This reflects evidentiary threshold rather than absence of legislative capacity.

Governance Structures in Mining

Mining corporations commonly operate with:

- Board-level safety oversight
- Executive safety dashboards
- Internal audit programs
- External technical review processes
- Regulator engagement mechanisms

These structures do not prevent failure. However, they create evidentiary complexity.

Where officers can demonstrate structured oversight, prosecution must prove that those structures were knowingly ineffective or consciously ignored.

Such proof was not established in the reviewed mining matters.

The Exposure Horizon

The absence of officer convictions during 2015–2025 should not be interpreted as insulation.

If future evidence demonstrates:

- Repeated documented warnings ignored
- Board-level knowledge of escalating fatal probability
- Failure to allocate resources despite explicit risk identification
- Deliberate prioritisation of production over mitigation

The prosecutorial posture may change.

The decade examined establishes a baseline, not a ceiling.

Conclusion

Officer liability in mining during 2015–2025 was shaped by statutory due diligence requirements and criminal evidentiary standards.

Corporate entities were prosecuted following fatal incidents.

Officer prosecutions were comparatively rare.

No industrial manslaughter conviction was secured against a mining officer during this period.

The distinction lies between implementation failure and gross criminal negligence.

The statutory framework remains capable of imposing officer liability where evidence supports it.

The matters examined during this decade did not present that evidentiary matrix.

Chapter References

Brisbane Auto Recycling Pty Ltd; R v Jeffrey Owen [2020] QDC 113.

Office of the Work Health and Safety Prosecutor (Queensland) (2024) Carborough Downs Coal Management Pty Ltd fined following fatal underground incident.

WorkSafe Western Australia (2024) Prosecution commenced – Karlawinda Mine fatal collision.

WorkSafe Western Australia (2025) RUC Mining Contractors Pty Ltd fined following underground fatality at Hamlet mine.

Work Health and Safety Act 2020 (WA), s 27, ss 30A–30B.

Work Health and Safety Act 2011 (Qld), s 27, s 34C.

Work Health and Safety Act 2011 (NSW), s 27.

CHAPTER 9

Category 1 Reckless Conduct: The Criminal Middle Ground

The work health and safety legislative framework establishes a graduated enforcement structure. Primary duty breaches sit at one end. Industrial manslaughter sits at the extreme.

Between those poles lies Category 1 reckless conduct.

Understanding why mining prosecutions during 2015–2025 rarely escalated to Category 1 is essential to understanding the absence of industrial manslaughter convictions.

Statutory Architecture

Under section 31 of the Work Health and Safety Act 2020 (WA) and section 31 of the Work Health and Safety Act 2011 (Qld), a Category 1 offence is committed where:

- A person has a health and safety duty, and
- The person, without reasonable excuse, engages in conduct that exposes an individual to a risk of death or serious injury or illness, and
- The person is reckless as to the risk.

Recklessness in criminal law requires subjective awareness of the risk and conscious disregard of it.

This is materially different from negligence.

Negligence concerns failure to take reasonable care.

Recklessness concerns conscious disregard of a known serious risk.

The Recklessness Threshold

Courts interpreting recklessness require evidence that:

- The accused knew of the risk of death or serious injury, and
- Proceeded with the conduct regardless.

The prosecution must establish that awareness beyond reasonable doubt.

This is a high evidentiary bar.

In mining prosecutions reviewed during 2015–2025, while serious hazards were foreseeable, evidence typically demonstrated system failure rather than conscious risk-taking.

Foreseeability is not recklessness.

General awareness of mining hazards is not equivalent to knowledge of imminent fatal risk in a specific configuration.

Mining Prosecution Patterns

Fatal mining prosecutions during this decade overwhelmingly proceeded under primary duty provisions rather than Category 1.

This reflects evidentiary realities.

In matters involving:

- Mobile plant interaction
- Ground collapse
- Gas management
- Mechanical isolation

Investigations generally revealed:

- Systems existed
- Risk assessments were conducted
- Controls were partially implemented
- Supervision was imperfect

What was absent was proof that duty holders consciously appreciated a specific fatal risk and chose to proceed regardless.

Without that proof, Category 1 charges are difficult to sustain.

Comparative Category 1 Prosecutions

Outside mining, Category 1 prosecutions have succeeded where:

- Defects were repeatedly identified
- Regulator notices were issued
- Explicit warnings were ignored
- Unsafe conduct continued despite knowledge

The contrast illustrates the difference between serious breach and reckless exposure.

Mining prosecutions during the examined period did not present evidentiary matrices demonstrating sustained conscious disregard.

Relationship to Industrial Manslaughter

Industrial manslaughter requires proof of criminal negligence, a threshold higher still than recklessness.

If Category 1 reckless conduct cannot be established, industrial manslaughter will almost certainly fail.

The absence of Category 1 convictions in mining fatality matters during 2015–2025 is therefore instructive.

It indicates that evidentiary proof of subjective awareness and disregard was not established.

Evidentiary Complexity in Mining

Mining environments are technically complex.

Fatal incidents frequently arise from:

- Multi-factor interaction
- Equipment failure
- Human error
- Communication lapse
- Environmental variability

Where causation is multi-factorial, isolating a conscious decision to expose a worker to fatal risk is difficult.

Prosecutors must prove not merely that better systems were available, but that the accused appreciated a specific fatal risk and proceeded regardless.

That burden is substantial.

The Structural Position of Category 1

Category 1 offences occupy a critical structural position in the enforcement ladder.

They represent:

- More than breach
- Less than industrial manslaughter

The relative absence of Category 1 mining convictions during this decade reinforces the evidentiary strength required to move beyond primary duty breach.

Conclusion

Category 1 reckless conduct requires proof of subjective awareness of risk and conscious disregard.

Between 2015 and 2025, mining fatality prosecutions did not establish that threshold.

Serious breaches occurred.

Recklessness, in the criminal sense, was not proven.

This evidentiary reality explains the absence of industrial manslaughter convictions within the sector during the period examined.

Chapter References

Work Health and Safety Act 2020 (WA), s 31.

Work Health and Safety Act 2011 (Qld), s 31.

Work Health and Safety Act 2011 (NSW), s 31.

Brisbane Auto Recycling Pty Ltd; R v Jeffrey Owen [2020] QDC 113.

CHAPTER 10

Industrial Manslaughter in Australia: Legislative Design, Criminal Negligence and the Mining Absence

Industrial manslaughter provisions were introduced across several Australian jurisdictions to address workplace deaths involving criminal negligence. These provisions represent the highest tier of statutory criminal liability under work health and safety legislation.

Between 2015 and 2025, industrial manslaughter charges were laid in multiple sectors. No conviction was secured in relation to a mining fatality during this period.

Understanding this pattern requires examination of legislative structure and judicial application.

Western Australia

Industrial manslaughter provisions were introduced into Western Australian law through amendments to the Work Health and Safety Act 2020 (WA).

Section 30A creates the offence of industrial manslaughter – crime, applicable where:

- A person has a health and safety duty, and
- The person engages in conduct that causes the death of an individual, and
- The conduct constitutes gross negligence.

Section 30B creates industrial manslaughter – simple offence, applying where a duty holder engages in conduct that causes death and fails to comply with the duty, without requiring proof of gross negligence.

Gross negligence in criminal law requires a severe departure from the standard of care expected in the circumstances. It is more than carelessness. It requires proof of conduct so far below reasonable standards that it warrants criminal punishment.

Between commencement of the Act and 2025, no industrial manslaughter conviction arose from a mining fatality in Western Australia.

Queensland

Queensland introduced industrial manslaughter provisions in 2017 through amendments to the Work Health and Safety Act 2011 (Qld). Section 34C establishes the offence.

The offence applies where:

- A worker dies in the course of carrying out work, and
- The person conducting the business or undertaking causes the death through negligent conduct.

The Queensland provisions extend liability to senior officers.

The first industrial manslaughter conviction under the Queensland WHS framework occurred in 2020 in R v Jeffrey Owen; Brisbane Auto Recycling Pty Ltd [2020] QDC 113.

In that matter, a worker was fatally crushed by a forklift. The sentencing court found that the company and its director had engaged in prolonged disregard of safety obligations despite awareness of fatal risk. The director was sentenced to imprisonment.

The evidentiary findings included repeated unsafe practices, prior warnings and absence of meaningful corrective action.

No equivalent industrial manslaughter conviction arose from a mining fatality during the examined decade.

Criminal Negligence Threshold

Industrial manslaughter requires proof of criminal negligence.

Criminal negligence involves:

- A duty of care
- A breach of that duty
- Causation of death
- Conduct constituting a gross departure from reasonable standards

This is a higher threshold than:

- Primary duty breach
- Category 1 reckless conduct

It requires proof that the accused's conduct was so deficient that it warrants criminal sanction.

In the mining prosecutions reviewed in earlier chapters, evidence established implementation failures, supervision deficiencies and control weaknesses.

What was not established was gross departure accompanied by criminal indifference.

Mining Fatalities 2015–2025: Structural Characteristics

Fatal mining incidents during this period frequently involved:

- Multi-factor causation
- Engineering system interaction
- Operational error
- Communication lapse
- Environmental variability

Where causation is multi-factorial and governance structures exist, establishing criminal negligence against officers or corporations becomes evidentially complex.

This does not reduce seriousness. It increases prosecutorial burden.

The Absence of Mining IM Convictions

The absence of industrial manslaughter convictions in mining during 2015–2025 reflects several intersecting realities:

1. Governance structures in mining corporations are typically formalised and documented.
2. Fatal incidents often arise from implementation breakdown rather than systemic abandonment.
3. Proof of executive-level gross negligence requires clear evidence of conscious disregard.
4. Prosecutorial discretion aligns charges with provable thresholds.

The statutory framework remains available. The evidentiary matrix required to satisfy it has not been established in mining cases during the examined period.

Distinguishing Serious Breach from Criminal Conduct

It is legally significant to distinguish between:

- Serious system failure
- Reckless exposure
- Criminal negligence

Mining prosecutions during 2015–2025 demonstrated serious breach.

They did not demonstrate gross departure from reasonable standards at the level required for industrial manslaughter.

The difference lies not in moral weight, but in evidentiary sufficiency.

Conclusion

Industrial manslaughter provisions in Western Australia and Queensland provide mechanisms for imposing criminal liability for workplace deaths arising from gross negligence.

Between 2015 and 2025:

- Industrial manslaughter convictions were secured in non-mining sectors.
- No mining fatality resulted in an industrial manslaughter conviction.

This pattern reflects the criminal negligence threshold embedded in the legislation.

The statutory boundary remains evidentiary, not rhetorical.

Chapter References

Work Health and Safety Act 2020 (WA), ss 30A–30B.

Work Health and Safety Act 2011 (Qld), s 34C.

R v Jeffrey Owen; Brisbane Auto Recycling Pty Ltd [2020] QDC 113.

Queensland Government (2017) Work Health and Safety and Other Legislation Amendment Act 2017.

CHAPTER 11

Industrial Manslaughter and Mining: Why the Threshold Has Not Been Crossed

The preceding chapters examined fatal mining prosecutions between 2015 and 2025 across Western Australia and Queensland. Corporate convictions were secured in multiple matters involving mobile plant interaction, ground control failure and hazardous atmosphere management.

Category 1 reckless conduct prosecutions were rare.

Industrial manslaughter convictions did not occur in relation to mining fatalities during this period.

This chapter examines why.

Structural Conditions in Mining

Mining differs from many other industries in several legally significant respects.

Operations are typically characterised by:

- Formalised safety management systems
- Board-level safety oversight
- Dedicated health and safety personnel
- Internal audit programs
- Regulatory inspection regimes
- Engineering risk assessments

These features do not prevent fatal incidents. They do, however, create an evidentiary environment in which systemic abandonment of safety is difficult to prove.

Industrial manslaughter requires proof of gross negligence. Where governance systems are demonstrably present, prosecution must establish that those systems were either knowingly ineffective or consciously disregarded.

During the decade examined, mining prosecutions demonstrated implementation failure rather than systemic abdication.

Implementation Failure Versus Criminal Indifference

The prosecutions reviewed in Chapters 3–6 reveal consistent patterns:

- Traffic management plans existed but were imperfectly enforced.
- Ground support systems were designed but not fully verified.
- Gas monitoring infrastructure was present but escalation was deficient.
- Mechanical isolation procedures were documented but inconsistently applied.

These failures were serious. Courts imposed significant fines.

However, criminal negligence requires more than serious failure.

It requires proof that conduct represented a gross departure from reasonable standards, accompanied by disregard for the safety of others.

The evidence in the reviewed mining matters did not demonstrate that decision-makers consciously appreciated an imminent fatal probability and proceeded regardless.

The Knowledge Barrier

Industrial manslaughter prosecutions require clear evidentiary linkage between:

- Knowledge of risk,
- Failure to act, and
- Causation of death.

In mining fatality cases during this period, evidence generally demonstrated that:

- Hazards were recognised at a general level.
- Risk assessments were conducted.
- Mitigation strategies were identified.
- Governance reporting mechanisms existed.

What was absent was proof that officers or corporate decision-makers possessed specific knowledge of an imminent fatal hazard in the configuration that ultimately caused death and chose not to intervene.

The distinction between general hazard awareness and imminent fatal probability is legally decisive.

Multi-Factor Causation

Mining fatalities frequently arise from multiple interacting factors.

These may include:

- Equipment limitations
- Environmental conditions
- Human error
- Communication lapse
- Localised supervision breakdown

Where causation is multi-factorial, isolating a single executive decision as constituting gross criminal negligence becomes more complex.

This complexity increases prosecutorial burden.

In the absence of evidence demonstrating conscious disregard of fatal probability, prosecution under primary duty provisions remains the more appropriate statutory pathway.

Regulatory Strategy and Charge Selection

Regulators select charges based on available evidence.

Primary duty offences require proof that a duty holder failed to ensure safety so far as reasonably practicable.

Category 1 offences require proof of recklessness.

Industrial manslaughter requires proof of criminal negligence.

The reviewed mining matters supported breach findings. They did not support findings of subjective recklessness or gross departure.

Charge selection reflected evidentiary sufficiency.

Comparison with Non-Mining Industrial Manslaughter

The Queensland industrial manslaughter conviction in R v Jeffrey Owen; Brisbane Auto Recycling Pty Ltd [2020] QDC 113 demonstrates the contrast.

In that matter, the court found:

- Repeated unsafe practices
- Prior regulatory engagement
- Absence of effective safety systems
- Prolonged disregard of known fatal risk

The evidentiary profile included clear proof of awareness and sustained indifference.

The mining prosecutions examined during 2015–2025 did not present equivalent matrices.

The difference is not industry identity. It is evidentiary structure.

Chapter References

Work Health and Safety Act 2020 (WA), ss 30A–30B.

Work Health and Safety Act 2011 (Qld), s 34C.

R v Jeffrey Owen; Brisbane Auto Recycling Pty Ltd [2020] QDC 113.

Queensland Government (2017) Work Health and Safety and Other Legislation Amendment Act 2017.

CHAPTER 12

The Decade in Synthesis: What Mining Prosecutions 2015–2025 Actually Reveal

Between 2015 and 2025, Australian mining fatalities did not disappear. Nor did prosecutions. Corporate convictions were secured across hazard domains including mobile plant interaction, ground failure, mechanical isolation and gas management. Fines were imposed. Enforceable undertakings were accepted. Officers were scrutinised.

Yet one feature remained conspicuous.

Industrial manslaughter convictions in mining were absent.

To understand whether that absence reflects regulatory hesitation, legislative limitation, or evidentiary discipline, the decade must be assessed as a whole rather than through isolated hazard categories.

This chapter synthesises the prosecution patterns across Western Australia and Queensland, the two jurisdictions that provide the heaviest evidentiary dataset for the period examined.

The Structural Stability of Charging Decisions

Across both WA and QLD, the dominant charging pathway following fatal mining incidents was breach of primary duty provisions.

Under the Work Health and Safety Act 2011 (Qld), prosecutions proceeded primarily under section 32 (Category 2 – failure exposing an individual to risk of death or serious injury) or section 31

(Category 1 – reckless conduct) in limited non-mining contexts.

Under the Work Health and Safety Act 2020 (WA), the equivalent Category 2 and Category 1 provisions applied following harmonisation.

Industrial manslaughter provisions exist in both jurisdictions:

- Queensland: WHS Act 2011 (Qld), sections 34C–34D.
- Western Australia: WHS Act 2020 (WA), sections 30A–30B.

Despite these provisions, mining prosecutions during 2015–2025 did not culminate in officer industrial manslaughter convictions and did not produce the wave of IM litigation sometimes anticipated in public discourse.

The explanation lies not in absence of fatalities, but in the structure of proof.

Evidentiary Architecture Versus Political Narrative

Industrial manslaughter requires proof of criminal negligence.

This is not synonymous with serious breach.

Criminal negligence requires:

- A gross departure from the standard of care.
- Conduct meriting criminal punishment.
- Proof beyond reasonable doubt of that gross departure.

In mining prosecutions reviewed across WA and QLD during the decade examined, the evidentiary pattern was consistent:

1. Systems existed.
2. Hazards were known.
3. Controls were documented.
4. Implementation failed at operational level.
5. Governance structures were present but imperfect.

That profile supports conviction under breach provisions.

It does not automatically support proof of criminal indifference.

The difference is doctrinally significant.

The presence of board safety committees, internal audits, engineering reviews and regulator engagement complicates proof that officers consciously disregarded a known and imminent fatal risk.

Mining is not characterised by absence of safety architecture.

It is characterised by failure within complex systems.

That distinction materially influences charging decisions.

Western Australia: Post-Harmonisation Position

Western Australia harmonised its work health and safety framework in 2022. The WHS Act 2020 (WA) introduced industrial manslaughter provisions applicable to officers and corporate bodies.

However, fatal mining prosecutions during the early harmonisation period continued to reflect primary duty charging patterns.

Several factors contribute to this stability:

1. Transitional period following legislative reform.
2. Ongoing evidentiary caution in selecting IM charges.
3. Complexity of causation in mining incidents involving multiple technical factors.
4. Existence of layered governance structures within large mining corporations.

Regulator public statements emphasised seriousness of breaches and deterrence objectives, but sentencing outcomes continued to align with breach rather than criminal homicide frameworks.

This suggests prosecutorial calibration rather than timidity.

Queensland: The Earlier Industrial Manslaughter Jurisdiction

Queensland introduced industrial manslaughter provisions earlier than WA.

Despite this temporal advantage, mining did not generate a sequence of officer IM convictions during the period examined.

Queensland fatal mining matters during this decade frequently involved:

- Mobile plant interactions.
- Geotechnical failures.
- Maintenance isolation breakdowns.

Corporate prosecutions were pursued.

Officer prosecutions were comparatively rare.

The absence of officer IM convictions in mining is notable because Queensland has demonstrated willingness to pursue IM in other sectors.

This comparison is instructive.

Where IM charges have succeeded in Queensland outside mining, the evidentiary pattern often included:

- Repeated regulator notices.
- Explicit knowledge of life-threatening conditions.
- Clear refusal to rectify.
- Documented disregard over time.

Mining prosecutions during 2015–2025 did not present that evidentiary profile at executive level.

This does not minimise seriousness of the incidents.

It clarifies the criminal threshold.

Implementation Failure Versus Systemic Absence

Across hazard domains analysed in earlier chapters, a recurring distinction emerges:

Failures were implementation failures.

They were not characterised by complete absence of safety systems.

In mobile plant cases:

- Traffic management plans existed.
- Training occurred.
- Near miss reporting systems were in place.
- Physical engineering solutions were incomplete or inadequately enforced.

In ground control matters:

- Geotechnical plans existed.
- Support standards were documented.
- Risk assessments were conducted.
- Supervision and trigger escalation were deficient.

In gas management cases:

- Monitoring infrastructure existed.
- Trigger action response plans were documented.
- Calibration and withdrawal enforcement faltered.

The law does not criminalise imperfection.

It criminalises gross indifference.

That boundary was not crossed in the mining matters examined during this decade.

The Officer Liability Horizon

Officer due diligence provisions require:

- Knowledge acquisition.
- Resource allocation.
- Process verification.
- Compliance monitoring.

In the prosecutions reviewed, officers could generally demonstrate:

- Formal reporting structures.
- Safety dashboards.
- Internal audit programs.
- Regulator engagement.
- Board oversight committees.

These structures did not prevent fatalities.

However, they created evidentiary barriers to proving criminal negligence.

The decade examined therefore illustrates a practical exposure horizon:

Officer industrial manslaughter liability in mining will likely require:

1. Documented executive awareness of escalating fatal probability.
2. Repeated ignored engineering recommendations.
3. Explicit prioritisation of production over known fatal hazard mitigation.
4. Absence or falsification of governance mechanisms.

That evidentiary matrix did not arise in the matters prosecuted between 2015 and 2025.

Regulatory Restraint or Evidentiary Discipline?

A common critique suggests regulators hesitate to prosecute industrial manslaughter against large mining entities due to political or economic sensitivity.

The decade examined does not support that conclusion.

Regulators pursued substantial fines.

Convictions were secured.

Detailed sentencing remarks criticised systemic shortcomings.

The absence of IM convictions aligns more coherently with evidentiary discipline than with regulatory reluctance.

Industrial manslaughter is a criminal offence of high gravity.

Over-charging without evidentiary sufficiency risks acquittal and jurisprudential weakening of the provision.

The prosecution patterns during this decade reflect strategic calibration.

Comparative Sectoral Observations

Mining differs from certain other sectors in structural characteristics:

- High capital intensity.
- Formalised engineering oversight.
- Established regulatory inspection regimes.
- Sophisticated internal safety management systems.

Sectors where industrial manslaughter convictions have occurred often involve smaller entities with limited governance infrastructure or prolonged documented non-compliance.

Mining fatalities during 2015–2025 occurred within systems that were documented, audited and externally scrutinised.

The failures were serious.

They were not legally characterised as abandonment of safety responsibility.

The Decade as Baseline

The period 2015–2025 should be understood as a baseline decade.

It demonstrates:

- The judiciary's fidelity to evidentiary thresholds.

- The durability of the reasonably practicable standard.
- The distinction between breach and criminal negligence.
- The continued primacy of engineering controls in judicial reasoning.
- The prosecutorial caution surrounding industrial manslaughter.

This baseline does not preclude future escalation.

Technological advancement, data analytics and enhanced monitoring may reduce evidentiary ambiguity in future cases.

As proximity detection, real-time gas modelling and predictive analytics mature, failure to implement mature technology may alter reasonably practicable analysis.

Future prosecutions may therefore reflect shifting expectations.

What the Decade Proves

When the hazard domains are synthesised and charging decisions are examined collectively, the decade proves five central propositions:

1. Mining fatalities continue to arise from known hazard domains.
2. Corporate prosecutions remain the dominant accountability mechanism.
3. Officer liability is bounded by proof of knowledge and verification failure.
4. Industrial manslaughter requires evidence of gross departure, not serious breach alone.
5. Prosecutorial restraint aligns with criminal law standards rather than institutional hesitation.

This is not a narrative of leniency.

It is a narrative of evidentiary precision.

Conclusion

Between 2015 and 2025, mining prosecutions across Western Australia and Queensland reveal a consistent doctrinal boundary.

The reasonably practicable standard remains the principal accountability framework.

Corporate entities were held liable where systems failed.

Officers were scrutinised but not criminally convicted in the absence of proof of gross negligence.

Industrial manslaughter provisions exist and remain available.

The decade examined demonstrates that they will be deployed where the evidentiary matrix justifies their use.

Mining fatalities during this period were tragic.

They were legally serious.

They were prosecuted.

They did not, in the matters reviewed, satisfy the criminal threshold of industrial manslaughter.

The line between breach and crime remained intact.

That is the central lesson of the decade.

Chapter References

Work Health and Safety Act 2011 (Qld)
Work Health and Safety Act 2020 (WA)
Queensland Resources Safety and Health Act 2020 (Qld)
Explanatory Notes, Work Health and Safety and Other Legislation Amendment Act 2017 (Qld)
Safe Work Australia, Model Work Health and Safety Act
Sentencing remarks and publicly available prosecution summaries from:

- Department of Mines, Industry Regulation and Safety (WA)
- Resources Safety and Health Queensland
- WorkSafe Queensland
- Supreme and District Court sentencing transcripts (WA and Qld, 2015–2025 mining matters)

CHAPTER 13

The Future Exposure Horizon: Technology, Data and Escalating Expectations

The decade between 2015 and 2025 demonstrates doctrinal stability. Industrial manslaughter provisions were introduced or strengthened. Fatalities occurred. Corporate prosecutions were secured. Officer criminal convictions were rare. The boundary between breach and gross negligence remained intact.

The question that follows is not whether that boundary will disappear.

It is whether evolving operational and technological conditions will move it.

Mining is not static. Control expectations evolve alongside technological maturity. What was once aspirational may become reasonably practicable. What was once technically unavailable may become standard.

That shift matters because the reasonably practicable analysis is dynamic.

Technological Maturation and the Reasonably Practicable Standard

Across hazard domains examined earlier, a common feature emerged: engineering controls existed but were imperfectly implemented. Proximity detection systems were available but not universally deployed. Real-time geotechnical monitoring systems were present but inconsistently escalated. Gas monitoring infrastructure existed but calibration and enforcement faltered.

As these technologies mature, the evidentiary analysis changes.

A control that is:
- commercially available
- operationally reliable
- integrated into peer operations
- cost-proportionate to risk

will increasingly be treated by courts as reasonably practicable.

The maturation of collision avoidance systems in mobile plant fleets illustrates this shift. Early in the decade, questions of suitability and integration were prominent. By the latter half, such systems became embedded in large operations.

Future prosecutions may therefore treat failure to implement mature detection technology differently from earlier matters.

The law does not stand still. It calibrates to technical feasibility.

Data, Predictive Analytics and Knowledge Attribution

Another structural shift concerns data visibility.

Mining corporations increasingly operate with:

- centralised safety dashboards
- near miss analytics
- predictive maintenance data
- geotechnical modelling outputs
- real-time atmospheric monitoring

When risk signals are aggregated and escalated at executive level, knowledge attribution becomes clearer.

During 2015–2025, many prosecutions revealed systemic knowledge of hazard categories, but not documented executive awareness of imminent fatal risk in a specific configuration.

If predictive analytics begin identifying high-probability fatal trajectories — and those alerts are recorded at board level — the evidentiary threshold may narrow.

Officer liability hinges on knowledge and response.

In an era of high-resolution safety data, plausible deniability diminishes.

The more visible the risk, the higher the expectation of escalation.

Governance Formalisation and Its Limits

Mining corporations are characterised by formal governance structures. Safety committees, audit programs and board oversight mechanisms were frequently cited in sentencing remarks during the decade examined.

These structures shielded officers from criminal conviction not because they prevented failure, but because they complicated proof of gross indifference.

However, governance structures must remain substantive rather than ceremonial.

If future prosecutions reveal:

- internal audit findings documenting escalating fatal exposure
- repeated budget deferral of critical engineering controls
- board-level awareness of control breakdown
- continuation of production without interim mitigation

the doctrinal stability observed during 2015–2025 may not persist.

The decade examined does not immunise the future.

It establishes a baseline.

Industrial Manslaughter as a Dormant Instrument

Industrial manslaughter provisions in WA and QLD have not been extensively deployed in mining during the decade examined.

That absence does not render them symbolic.

It renders them contingent.

Industrial manslaughter functions as a reserve instrument. It is engaged where the evidentiary matrix justifies criminal condemnation rather than regulatory sanction.

Mining prosecutions between 2015 and 2025 demonstrate that regulators will pursue breach where systems fail.

They do not demonstrate that regulators will refrain from IM where gross negligence can be proven.

The absence of past conviction does not predict future restraint.

It reflects historical evidence.

Sectoral Comparison and Escalation Risk

Comparison with non-mining industrial manslaughter matters reveals a consistent theme: conviction follows documented disregard.

Where repeated regulator notices were ignored. Where lethal conditions were known and tolerated. Where warnings were explicit and action absent.

Mining has not, in the matters examined, produced that evidentiary clarity at executive level.

But as hazard signals become increasingly quantifiable and documented in digital systems, the threshold for proving awareness may shift.

Future exposure is therefore a function not of legislative change, but of evidentiary traceability.

Conclusion

The decade examined demonstrates doctrinal stability.

The next decade may test it.

Technological maturation, predictive data systems and heightened governance transparency narrow the space between systemic failure and provable criminal negligence.

The legal boundary remains high.

But the evidentiary path to that boundary is becoming clearer.

End of Chapter References

Work Health and Safety Act 2011 (Qld)
Work Health and Safety Act 2020 (WA)
Safe Work Australia, Model Work Health and Safety Act
Resources Safety and Health Queensland, annual safety performance reports
Department of Mines, Industry Regulation and Safety (WA), safety performance publications
Public sentencing remarks, mining fatality matters (WA and Qld, 2015–2025)

CHAPTER 14

The Boundary Between Breach and Crime

Across mobile plant interaction, ground instability, mechanical isolation and gas management, a pattern has emerged.

Mining fatalities during 2015–2025 were prosecuted.

Corporate liability was established.

Fines were imposed.

Industrial manslaughter convictions did not materialise.

The significance of that pattern lies not in absence of accountability, but in preservation of legal distinction.

The Function of the Criminal Threshold

Criminal law carries moral condemnation.

It requires proof not merely of error, but of gross departure from acceptable standards.

The reasonably practicable standard governs breach. It balances likelihood, consequence, knowledge, availability and cost.

Industrial manslaughter requires something more.

It requires conduct so far below acceptable standard that it warrants criminal punishment.

The decade examined illustrates judicial fidelity to that distinction.

Serious breach was punished.

Criminal negligence was not presumed.

The Persistence of Known Hazards

Mobile plant interactions remain foreseeable.
Ground instability remains technically complex.
Mechanical isolation failures persist.
Gas management remains catastrophic in potential.

The recurrence of hazard does not equate to criminal indifference.

It reflects the inherent risk profile of mining.

The legal system recognises that high-risk industries cannot eliminate all hazard. They are required to manage it to a reasonably practicable level.

Where management fails, breach liability follows.

Where management demonstrates gross indifference, crime follows.

That distinction has endured.

Evidentiary Discipline as Institutional Strength

Some observers interpret absence of industrial manslaughter convictions in mining as regulatory caution.

A more rigorous interpretation is evidentiary discipline.

Criminal provisions lose authority when deployed without sufficient proof.

The decade examined demonstrates prosecutorial selection grounded in sufficiency of evidence rather than symbolic severity.

That restraint reinforces legitimacy.

The Continuing Relevance of Reasonably Practicable

Throughout this manuscript, one statutory phrase recurs.

Reasonably practicable.

It remains the operative core of work health and safety law.

The courts have applied it with technical precision:

- examining engineering feasibility
- evaluating proportionality of cost
- assessing availability of controls
- scrutinising implementation and supervision

The standard has not been diluted by introduction of industrial manslaughter.

It has remained central.

What This Book Ultimately Establishes

This examination of mining prosecutions between 2015 and 2025 establishes several conclusions:

1. Fatal mining incidents continue to arise from identifiable hazard domains.
2. Corporate prosecutions remain the primary accountability mechanism.
3. Officer liability is constrained by knowledge and verification thresholds.
4. Industrial manslaughter provisions are present but contingent on proof of gross negligence.
5. The legal boundary between breach and crime remains doctrinally stable.

These findings are not ideological.

They are evidentiary.

The Role of Future Leadership

The next phase of mining accountability will not be shaped solely by legislation.

It will be shaped by leadership response to evolving expectations.

Executives who treat safety dashboards as operational intelligence rather than compliance artefacts reduce exposure.

Those who ignore quantifiable risk signals may narrow the distance between breach and crime.

The line exists.

It is visible.

It is evidentiary.

Conclusion

Between 2015 and 2025, mining prosecutions across Western Australia and Queensland demonstrate the resilience of legal principle.

Corporate breaches were punished.

Industrial manslaughter was reserved for cases meeting the criminal threshold.

The absence of officer IM convictions in mining during this decade does not signify weakness.

It signifies boundary maintenance.

The criminal law has not retreated.

It has waited for proof.

If future evidence satisfies that threshold, the provisions are ready.

Until then, the doctrine remains clear:

Not every fatal breach is a crime.

But where the evidence demonstrates gross indifference to life, the law will respond accordingly.

Chapter References

Work Health and Safety Act 2011 (Qld)
Work Health and Safety Act 2020 (WA)

Queensland Resources Safety and Health Act 2020 (Qld)
Safe Work Australia, Model Work Health and Safety Act
Department of Mines, Industry Regulation and Safety (WA) – Prosecution summaries
Resources Safety and Health Queensland – Prosecution summaries
Selected Supreme and District Court sentencing remarks (WA and Qld mining fatality matters, 2015–2025)

CHAPTER 15

Governance in Practice: What Mining Officers and Boards Must Now Do

The preceding chapters examined mining prosecutions between 2015 and 2025 across Western Australia and Queensland. They analysed hazard domains, charging patterns, officer liability thresholds and the boundary between breach and criminal negligence.

The decade established doctrinal stability.

Corporate prosecutions were secured.

Industrial manslaughter remained reserved for cases meeting a high evidentiary threshold.

The question that now matters is not what courts have done.

It is what officers and boards must do in response.

This chapter translates the decade's legal lessons into practical governance implications.

---

1. Stop Treating Safety Reporting as Assurance

Across fatal mining prosecutions examined in this book, a recurring theme appeared:

Safety systems existed.

Dashboards were produced.

Audit processes operated.

But implementation faltered.

The existence of documentation did not prevent liability.

For officers, the lesson is clear:

Reporting is not verification.

A board that receives monthly safety dashboards without interrogating control effectiveness risks mistaking visibility for assurance.

Verification requires asking:

- How are exclusion zones physically enforced in mobile plant areas?
- How often are trigger action response plans stress-tested?
- What is the latency between near miss reporting and engineering intervention?
- Are high-risk intersections redesigned or merely re-briefed?

The decade demonstrates that courts examine implementation, not paper architecture.

---

2. Engineer Before You Instruct

Judicial reasoning across mobile plant and ground failure matters consistently prioritised engineering controls over administrative reliance.

Officers should therefore apply a simple internal governance rule:

Where fatal consequence is foreseeable, administrative controls alone are unlikely to satisfy reasonably practicable expectations if engineering solutions are available.

Boards should ask:

- What physical separation exists between heavy and light vehicles?
- Where blind geometry persists, what redesign options have been costed?
- Where proximity detection technology is mature, why has it not been deployed?

• Where gas thresholds are exceeded, what hard interlocks prevent restart?

The legal system does not require perfection.

It does expect proportionate engineering response to known fatal hazards.

---

3. Treat Near Miss Data as Escalation Signals

Near miss evidence featured prominently in sentencing remarks during the decade examined.

While near miss records did not elevate matters to industrial manslaughter, they contributed to foreseeability findings.

For governance purposes, near miss data is not merely operational feedback.

It is potential evidentiary material.

Boards should require:

• Aggregated analysis of high-energy interaction near misses.
• Trend analysis across sites.
• Time-to-control metrics following serious near miss events.
• Clear documentation of engineering escalation decisions.

If future prosecutions reveal repeated near misses with documented board awareness and no corrective engineering intervention, the officer exposure landscape may change.

Near misses are early warning systems.

Ignoring them narrows the legal buffer between breach and gross negligence.

---

4. Resource Allocation Must Be Traceable

Due diligence includes ensuring appropriate resources are available and used.

The decade examined revealed that where corporations could demonstrate investment in safety systems, officer prosecutions struggled to prove criminal negligence.

This does not mean expenditure equals immunity.

It means traceable, rational allocation decisions matter.

Boards should be able to demonstrate:

- Capital expenditure decisions relating to hazard mitigation.
- Risk-based prioritisation frameworks.
- Documented responses to engineering recommendations.
- Transparent treatment of deferred safety projects.

The critical question is not whether every risk can be eliminated.

It is whether decisions can withstand retrospective scrutiny.

---

5. Understand the Industrial Manslaughter Boundary

The decade examined clarifies the evidentiary boundary between breach and criminal negligence.

Industrial manslaughter in mining would likely require:

- Documented executive awareness of escalating fatal probability.
- Explicit warnings of imminent catastrophic risk.
- Repeated refusal to implement feasible controls.
- Evidence of prioritising production over safety mitigation.

Officers should not treat this as a comfort threshold.

They should treat it as a stress-test scenario.

Boards should periodically ask:

If this incident occurred tomorrow, what documentary record would prosecutors review?

What would that record reveal about our decision-making?

Governance is not merely about compliance.

It is about documentary resilience.

---

6. Move From Reactive Compliance to Predictive Control

The technological maturation discussed in Chapter 13 introduces a new governance expectation.

Predictive analytics, real-time monitoring and centralised dashboards increase visibility of risk.

With visibility comes responsibility.

Officers should ensure:

- Real-time gas exceedance alerts are escalated beyond operational teams.
- High-risk geotechnical modelling outputs are reviewed at executive level.
- Collision avoidance system data is analysed for pattern recognition.
- Fatigue analytics are integrated into operational decision-making.

The greater the data clarity, the more difficult it becomes to argue ignorance.

Governance must evolve with information availability.

---

7. Preserve the Boundary by Respecting It

One of the central findings of this book is that the boundary between breach and crime remained intact during 2015–2025.

That boundary was preserved not by leniency, but by evidentiary discipline.

Mining officers should not interpret absence of industrial manslaughter convictions as structural protection.

They should interpret it as proof that the criminal threshold is real.

The most reliable way to avoid crossing it is simple:

Act before escalation becomes obvious.

When engineering advice identifies critical vulnerability, respond.

When risk trends increase, intervene.

When technology matures, reassess control adequacy.

The law does not punish hindsight.

It punishes documented indifference.

---

8. The Governance Checklist Emerging From the Decade

Without reducing this analysis to simplistic formula, the decade suggests that prudent mining governance now includes:

- Active interrogation of engineering controls in fatal hazard domains.
- Structured escalation of serious near miss trends.
- Transparent documentation of safety investment decisions.
- Board-level review of trigger action compliance performance.
- Integration of predictive data into executive oversight.
- Independent verification of control effectiveness.

These are not aspirational measures.

They are consistent with how courts evaluate reasonably practicable control implementation.

Conclusion

Between 2015 and 2025, mining prosecutions in Western Australia and Queensland reveal a stable legal architecture.

Corporate entities were held accountable.

Industrial manslaughter provisions remained available but were not deployed absent evidentiary justification.

The lesson for officers and boards is not that risk has diminished.

It is that accountability is traceable.

Governance in the modern mining environment must be:

Documented.

Interrogative.
Engineering-focused.
Escalation-aware.
Technologically informed.

The law has demonstrated its patience.

It has not demonstrated tolerance for indifference.

The boundary remains clear.

Leadership determines how close to that boundary an organisation chooses to operate.

CHAPTER 16

Quantitative Enforcement Patterns in Mining Fatalities (2015–2025)

1. Why Quantitative Analysis Matters

Narrative accounts of mining fatalities are powerful, but enforcement patterns cannot be understood through anecdote alone. A decade of prosecutions across Western Australia and Queensland reveals structural consistency in charging decisions, penalty calibration and officer exposure.

This chapter steps back from individual hazard domains and examines enforcement numerically. The objective is not to reduce human loss to statistics, but to identify prosecutorial patterns and the evidentiary architecture that shaped them.

Between 2015 and 2025, both jurisdictions experienced mining fatalities across mobile plant interaction, ground failure, mechanical isolation and gas management. Corporate prosecutions followed in a significant proportion of those matters. Industrial manslaughter convictions did not emerge within the mining sector during this period.

Understanding that outcome requires examination of:

- Fatality volumes
- Prosecution frequency
- Charge categorisation
- Penalty magnitude
- Corporate versus officer exposure

2. Fatality Overview (WA and QLD Focus)

Safe Work Australia data and state regulator reports confirm that mining fatalities during 2015–2025 remained lower than peak historical decades, but persistent across core hazard domains.

Fatal incidents during the decade predominantly involved:

- Vehicle interaction and mobile plant
- Falls of ground and strata failure
- Mechanical maintenance and energy isolation
- Explosive and gas-related incidents

While precise annual numbers varied, neither WA nor QLD experienced sustained fatality escalation during this period. Fatal events occurred intermittently rather than in clustered catastrophic series.

This matters legally.

Industrial manslaughter prosecutions are more likely where systemic failure produces repeated warnings ignored over time. The fatality distribution during this decade was episodic rather than sequential within individual sites.

---

3. Corporate Prosecution Frequency

Regulator media releases and annual enforcement reports indicate that corporate entities were prosecuted in a substantial proportion of fatal mining matters.

Patterns observed include:

- Primary duty charges under mining-specific legislation prior to harmonisation
- Category 2 offences under harmonised WHS frameworks
- Rare Category 1 (reckless) charges in mining fatality matters
- No industrial manslaughter convictions within the sector

The majority of fatal mining prosecutions proceeded under breach-based provisions rather than criminal negligence frameworks.

This reflects prosecutorial calibration rather than absence of statutory tools.

---

4. Charge Distribution Patterns

A review of publicly available prosecution summaries across WA and QLD demonstrates a consistent charging structure:

Category 2 Offences

Most mining fatality prosecutions were framed as failure to comply with health and safety duty exposing individuals to risk of death or serious injury.

These charges do not require proof of recklessness or gross negligence.

They require proof that:

- A duty existed
- The duty was breached
- The breach exposed a person to risk

This threshold is significantly lower than industrial manslaughter.

Category 1 (Reckless) Charges

In the mining fatality context, Category 1 charges were uncommon during the period examined.

Recklessness requires proof that the accused was aware of a substantial risk and unjustifiably disregarded it.

The evidentiary record in the prosecuted matters generally supported breach rather than subjective recklessness.

Industrial Manslaughter

Neither WA nor QLD secured an industrial manslaughter conviction in a mining fatality during this decade.

That absence is statistically significant given the size of the mining sector in both jurisdictions.

---

5. Corporate Versus Officer Charging Ratios

One of the most notable enforcement trends during 2015–2025 was the disparity between corporate and officer prosecutions.

Corporate entities were prosecuted frequently following fatal incidents.

Officer prosecutions were rare.

Industrial manslaughter charges against officers in mining did not result in conviction during the period examined.

This reflects the evidentiary complexity of establishing personal criminal negligence in environments where governance systems formally exist.

Publicly available records indicate that where officers were charged in mining contexts, the allegations focused on:

- Failure to exercise due diligence
- Failure to ensure adequate resources
- Failure to respond to known deficiencies

However, convictions required proof that the officer's conduct constituted a substantial departure from reasonable standards.

That threshold was rarely satisfied on publicly available evidence.

---

6. Penalty Magnitude and Fine Escalation

Sentencing remarks during the decade demonstrate increasing fine magnitude over time.

Early prosecutions within the period often resulted in substantial but comparatively moderate fines.

Later prosecutions, particularly under harmonised WHS frameworks, demonstrate:

- Higher maximum penalties
- Increased judicial commentary on deterrence

- Emphasis on general prevention
- Larger corporate fines

However, even as penalties increased, courts consistently differentiated between:

- Serious regulatory breach

and

- Criminal negligence

Fine magnitude does not equate to criminal classification.

Courts often imposed multi-million-dollar penalties under Category 2 frameworks without escalating to manslaughter.

---

7. Industrial Manslaughter Utilisation Outside Mining

During the same decade, industrial manslaughter convictions occurred in other sectors.

Those cases typically involved:

- Repeated documented warnings
- Direct supervisory knowledge of life-threatening conditions
- Explicit continuation of unsafe practices
- Absence of governance structure
- Small or medium enterprise environments

The contrast with mining is instructive.

Mining corporations typically operate with:

- Structured safety management systems
- Board-level reporting
- Regulatory inspection engagement
- Technical oversight

These structures do not prevent fatalities. But they complicate proof of gross negligence.

---

8. Evidentiary Threshold Indicators

Across the fatal mining prosecutions examined, the following elements were generally present:

- Known hazard category
- Identified control deficiencies
- Failure of implementation
- Exposure to fatal risk

The following elements were generally absent:

- Documented executive-level awareness of imminent fatal probability
- Explicit refusal to implement recommended engineering controls
- Repeated regulator prohibition notices ignored
- Written acceptance of fatal risk

Without such evidence, escalation to industrial manslaughter becomes legally fragile.

Prosecutors must assess not moral gravity but likelihood of conviction.

---

9. Near Miss Escalation Data

Mining operations record near miss data extensively.

However, publicly available prosecution records rarely demonstrate that near miss data reached a documented threshold indicating imminent fatality probability known to senior officers.

Near miss evidence supports foreseeability.

It does not automatically support criminal negligence.

For escalation to manslaughter, the evidentiary chain would need to show:

- Repeated pattern escalation
- Formal warning memoranda
- Clear engineering recommendations
- Deliberate deferral despite acknowledged lethal risk

The public record during this decade does not show that pattern in prosecuted matters.

---

10. Comparative WA–QLD Observations

While legislative language differs slightly between WA and QLD, enforcement patterns are strikingly consistent.

Both jurisdictions:

- Prosecuted corporate entities under breach provisions
- Rarely charged officers
- Did not secure mining industrial manslaughter convictions
- Emphasised deterrence in sentencing
- Relied heavily on hierarchy of control reasoning

This suggests structural rather than jurisdiction-specific factors.

---

11. The Statistical Boundary

The absence of industrial manslaughter convictions in mining during 2015–2025 cannot be dismissed as an anomaly.

Across:

- Multiple fatalities
- Multiple hazard domains
- Two major mining jurisdictions
- A full decade of enforcement

The prosecutorial boundary remained intact.

That statistical stability demands explanation.

It cannot be explained by regulatory weakness alone. It must be examined through evidentiary architecture.

---

12. Quantitative Conclusion

The decade examined reveals:

- Persistent mining fatalities
- Consistent corporate prosecutions
- Escalating penalty magnitude

- Rare officer charging
- No industrial manslaughter convictions

The enforcement data demonstrates that:

- Regulators are willing to prosecute
- Courts are willing to impose significant fines
- The criminal negligence threshold remains high

The mining sector during this period occupied a space between serious regulatory breach and criminal manslaughter.

That boundary is not accidental.

It is evidentiary.

The next chapter interrogates that boundary directly.

CHAPTER 17

The Evidentiary Boundary: Why Industrial Manslaughter Did Not Attach in Mining (2015–2025)

1. From Numbers to Threshold

Chapter 16 demonstrated a structural enforcement pattern across Western Australia and Queensland between 2015 and 2025:

- Fatalities occurred.
- Corporations were prosecuted.
- Penalties increased.
- Officer prosecutions were rare.
- Industrial manslaughter convictions did not emerge within mining.

The absence of industrial manslaughter convictions cannot be understood statistically alone. It requires examination of the evidentiary architecture underpinning the offence itself.

This chapter moves from quantitative observation to doctrinal analysis.

The question is not whether mining fatalities were serious. It is whether the available evidence in prosecuted matters met the criminal negligence threshold required by statute.

2. The Legal Architecture of Industrial Manslaughter

Industrial manslaughter provisions in Queensland and Western Australia require proof that:

- A duty existed.

- The duty was breached.
- The breach caused death.
- The conduct constituted criminal negligence (or gross negligence, depending on statutory wording).

The defining feature is not breach.

It is **gross departure**.

The criminal negligence standard requires proof that conduct represented such a serious departure from reasonable standards that it warrants criminal punishment.

This is not rhetorical elevation.

It is a historically entrenched criminal law principle.

The courts have long held that negligence becomes criminal only when it demonstrates such disregard for life and safety as to deserve punishment beyond regulatory sanction.

That distinction is fundamental.

---

3. Regulatory Breach Versus Criminal Negligence

Mining prosecutions during 2015–2025 clearly established regulatory breach in numerous matters.

Courts found that:

- Engineering controls were not implemented.
- Traffic management was inadequately enforced.
- Trigger action response plans were inconsistently applied.
- Isolation procedures were deficient.

These findings supported Category 2 convictions.

However, breach alone is insufficient for industrial manslaughter.

To escalate, prosecutors would need to prove:

- Awareness of a substantial and unjustifiable risk of death.
- Failure to act in the face of that awareness.
- A degree of disregard amounting to criminal indifference.

The evidentiary burden is not incremental.

It is exponential.

---

4. The Role of Foreseeability

Foreseeability in mining is rarely contested.

Mobile plant collisions are foreseeable.
Ground failure is foreseeable.
Gas ignition is foreseeable.

But foreseeability of hazard category is not equivalent to foreseeability of imminent death in a specific configuration.

Industrial manslaughter requires more than general industry knowledge.

It requires proof that the accused knew, or ought to have known, that death was a probable consequence of the specific conduct at issue.

The prosecuted matters during this decade demonstrated awareness of hazard types.

They did not consistently demonstrate awareness of imminent fatal inevitability.
That distinction is legally decisive.

---

5. Governance Complexity as Evidentiary Shield

Mining corporations typically operate within structured governance frameworks:

- Board-level safety reporting
- Internal audits
- Technical engineering oversight
- External inspections
- Documented risk registers

These structures do not eliminate risk.

However, they create evidentiary friction.

When prosecutors attempt to prove criminal negligence, defence counsel can demonstrate:

- Existence of systems
- Allocation of resources
- Active monitoring
- Continuous improvement efforts

Even if those systems failed in practice, their documented existence undermines arguments of gross indifference.

The presence of imperfect systems is often sufficient to prevent escalation to criminal negligence.

---

6. Officer Liability and Personal Criminal Exposure

Industrial manslaughter against officers requires proof that the officer's personal conduct constituted gross negligence.

This requires evidence of:

- Direct knowledge of escalating fatal risk
- Authority to intervene
- Failure to intervene
- Conscious disregard of consequence

In mining fatality prosecutions between 2015 and 2025, publicly available records do not demonstrate that senior officers:

- Ignored explicit engineering recommendations warning of imminent death
- Refused to fund critical safety controls despite documented lethal probability
- Suppressed internal fatal risk warnings

Without that chain, the prosecution faces substantial reasonable doubt.

---

7. The Production Pressure Narrative

Public discourse frequently attributes mining fatalities to production pressure.

Courts, however, require documentary proof.

Allegations that production was prioritised over safety must be supported by:

- Emails
- Board minutes
- Formal directives
- Written refusal of recommended controls

In the prosecuted matters during this period, sentencing remarks generally characterised failures as serious oversight deficiencies, not deliberate prioritisation of production over life.

Absent documentary evidence, motive remains speculative.

Speculation does not satisfy criminal standard.

---

8. Near Miss Escalation and Threshold Theory

Near miss events are legally relevant.

They establish knowledge of hazard manifestation.

However, to cross into criminal negligence, near miss evidence would need to demonstrate:

- Repeated pattern escalation
- Increasing severity indicators
- Formal executive awareness
- Failure to act despite recognised lethal trajectory

In the decade examined, near miss data supported foreseeability but did not demonstrate conscious disregard of imminent death probability.

That evidentiary escalation was not publicly documented.

---

9. Comparative Industrial Manslaughter Convictions Outside Mining

Where industrial manslaughter convictions have occurred in other sectors, common features include:

- Small enterprise environments
- Absence of formal safety systems
- Repeated regulator notices ignored
- Clear knowledge of immediate lethal conditions
- Continued operation despite prohibition warnings

The structural difference between such environments and large mining corporations is significant.

The criminal law threshold interacts differently with complex governance structures.

Mining's regulatory density does not eliminate risk, but it raises the evidentiary bar for criminal prosecution.

---

10. Parliamentary Intent Versus Judicial Application

Parliamentary debates introducing industrial manslaughter provisions emphasised:

- Stronger accountability
- Deterrence
- Cultural reform

However, courts remain bound by criminal standards of proof.

Judicial restraint is not opposition to legislative intent.

It is adherence to evidentiary discipline.

The absence of mining industrial manslaughter convictions during 2015–2025 reflects judicial fidelity to criminal law doctrine, not legislative failure.

---

11. The "Gross Departure" Test in Practice

The term "gross departure" requires examination of:

- Degree of deviation
- Duration of exposure
- Magnitude of known risk
- Availability of corrective measures
- Awareness of decision-makers

In mining prosecutions reviewed during this period, courts identified serious departures from expected standards.

They did not characterise those departures as gross in the criminal sense.

The difference is qualitative, not semantic.

---

12. What Would Have Crossed the Line?

Based on patterns observed, industrial manslaughter in mining would likely require evidence of:

- Documented internal fatal risk warnings
- Explicit engineering recommendations refused without justification
- Repeated high-level methane exceedances ignored
- Continued mobile plant interaction in known lethal configurations
- Executive-level awareness of escalating probability
- Failure to implement interim controls

Such an evidentiary matrix did not appear in the prosecuted matters examined during this decade.

---

13. The Stability of the Boundary

Across:

- Multiple fatalities
- Multiple hazard domains
- Two major jurisdictions
- A full decade of enforcement

The criminal boundary remained intact.

This stability suggests that:

- Regulators exercised charging restraint aligned with evidence
- Courts required demonstrable gross negligence
- Mining governance structures complicated escalation

The boundary was not accidental.

It was structural.

---

14. Normative Question: Should the Boundary Shift?

A deeper policy question arises:

Should industrial manslaughter attach more readily in complex corporate environments?

If the threshold were lowered, criminal law risks absorbing regulatory breach.

If the threshold remains high, public perception may view outcomes as insufficiently punitive.

This tension between deterrence and doctrinal integrity is central to modern work health and safety enforcement.

Mining sits at the heart of that debate.

---

15. Synthesis with Chapter 16

Chapter 16 demonstrated statistical stability.
This chapter explains doctrinal stability.

Together they demonstrate that:

- Industrial manslaughter provisions exist.
- Mining fatalities occurred.
- Prosecutors acted.
- Courts imposed significant penalties.
- Criminal negligence threshold remained un-crossed.

The absence of conviction is not absence of accountability.

It is evidence of evidentiary threshold.

Conclusion

Between 2015 and 2025, mining fatality prosecutions in Western Australia and Queensland reveal a consistent enforcement pattern:

Serious breach.
Significant penalty.
No criminal manslaughter conviction.

The distinction lies not in moral gravity but in proof.

Industrial manslaughter demands demonstrable gross departure.

The matters prosecuted during this decade did not present that matrix.

The boundary between regulatory breach and criminal negligence remains legally intact.

Whether it should remain so is a matter for legislative reconsideration, not judicial adjustment.

Chapter References

Work Health and Safety Act 2011 (Qld).

Work Health and Safety Act 2020 (WA).

Queensland Parliament (2017) Explanatory Notes: Work Health and Safety and Other Legislation Amendment Bill 2017.

Parliament of Western Australia (2019) Work Health and Safety Bill 2019 – Second Reading Speech.

Safe Work Australia (various years) Work-related Traumatic Injury Fatalities Reports.

Department of Mines, Industry Regulation and Safety (2015–2025) Prosecution Media Releases and Annual Reports.

Resources Safety and Health Queensland (2015–2025) Prosecution Summaries and Annual Reports

CHAPTER 18

Evidentiary Risk, Prosecutorial Discretion and the Limits of Public Data

1. The Gap Between Incident and Indictment

Fatal incidents generate immediate public reaction. Industrial manslaughter provisions amplify expectations of criminal accountability. Yet between incident and indictment lies a prosecutorial filtering process governed not by emotion, but by evidentiary sufficiency.

Prosecutors must ask:

- Is there a reasonable prospect of conviction?
- Can criminal negligence be proved beyond reasonable doubt?
- Is the evidence admissible and reliable?
- Can causation be established without ambiguity?

This filtering function shapes enforcement outcomes more than statutory maximum penalties.

In mining fatality prosecutions between 2015 and 2025, the decision not to pursue industrial manslaughter must be understood within this evidentiary context.

2. The Reasonable Prospect Test

Both Queensland and Western Australian prosecutorial authorities apply structured decision-making frameworks. A prosecution proceeds only where there is a reasonable prospect of conviction and where it is in the public interest.

The reasonable prospect test is evidence-driven.

It requires:

- Proof of duty
- Proof of breach
- Proof of causation
- Proof of gross negligence

Where evidence supports breach but not gross departure, escalation becomes legally precarious.

Industrial manslaughter charges that fail at trial weaken deterrence and undermine public confidence. Prosecutorial restraint is therefore not timidity. It is risk calibration.

---

3. The Burden of Proof Divide

Regulatory offences operate differently from criminal negligence.

Category 2 breaches require proof that a duty-holder failed to comply with a health and safety duty exposing a person to risk.

Industrial manslaughter requires proof of conduct so negligent as to warrant criminal sanction.

The difference is not incremental.

It is categorical.

Beyond reasonable doubt is a demanding standard. Where evidence permits multiple reasonable interpretations — system failure versus criminal indifference — acquittal risk increases substantially.

Mining fatality matters frequently involve multi-factor causation:

- Human error
- Engineering complexity
- Environmental conditions
- Supervisory oversight
- Communication lapse

This multiplicity complicates singular criminal attribution.

4. The Problem of Causation in Complex Systems

In high-reliability industries, fatalities rarely arise from a single conscious decision. They arise from layered system degradation.

Criminal law traditionally prefers identifiable acts or omissions.

Systemic drift does not always map cleanly onto individual culpability.

To prove industrial manslaughter in mining, prosecutors would need to demonstrate that:

- A specific decision-maker
- Knew of a specific lethal risk
- Failed to intervene
- And that failure directly caused death

Where causation involves interacting subsystems, evidentiary clarity diminishes.

This does not excuse failure. It complicates proof.

5. Documentary Evidence Threshold

Corporate prosecutions frequently rely on:

- Risk assessments
- Audit findings
- Training records
- Maintenance logs

For industrial manslaughter, documentation must show more than oversight.

It must show awareness of imminent lethal probability.

Absent:

- Explicit internal warnings
- Refused engineering recommendations
- Ignored prohibition notices

The prosecution's ability to demonstrate gross negligence weakens significantly.

Publicly available mining prosecutions during 2015–2025 do not reveal that level of documentary escalation.

6. Plea Negotiation and Charge Resolution

An additional factor rarely visible in public discourse is charge negotiation.

Corporate defendants may:

- Enter early guilty pleas
- Cooperate with investigation
- Undertake enforceable undertakings
- Demonstrate remediation

Early plea and cooperation reduce trial exposure.

Industrial manslaughter charges carry higher litigation risk and longer trial duration. Prosecutors must weigh resource allocation against evidentiary strength.

Charge calibration may therefore reflect litigation strategy rather than reluctance.

7. Public Data Limitations

This book relies on publicly available materials.

Regulator media releases and sentencing remarks do not disclose:

- Full internal correspondence
- Detailed witness examinations
- Legal advice provided to prosecutors
- Charge selection deliberations

Absence of industrial manslaughter conviction does not necessarily indicate absence of consideration.

It indicates absence of successful prosecution.

Transparency limitations must temper interpretation.

8. Risk of Overreach

Criminal law overreach carries consequences.

If industrial manslaughter were pursued without sufficient evidentiary foundation:

- Acquittal risk increases
- Precedent weakens prosecutorial authority
- Defence confidence strengthens

The stability observed between 2015 and 2025 may reflect cautious institutional learning.

---

9. Synthesis

The enforcement stability identified in Chapters 16 and 17 is not accidental.

It reflects:

- Prosecutorial risk assessment
- Criminal law thresholds
- Corporate governance complexity
- Evidentiary constraints

Industrial manslaughter is not a symbolic offence.

It is a high-burden criminal charge.

Mining prosecutions during this decade did not present sufficient evidence to reliably cross that boundary.

Chapter References

Work Health and Safety Act 2011 (Qld).
Work Health and Safety Act 2020 (WA).
Director of Public Prosecutions (Qld) – Guidelines for Prosecutors.
Office of the Director of Public Prosecutions (WA) – Prosecution Policy and Guidelines.
Safe Work Australia – Model WHS Act.

CHAPTER 19

Criminal Negligence in Australian Law: Doctrinal Foundations and Corporate Application

1. Why Doctrinal Context Matters

Chapters 16 through 18 established that industrial manslaughter did not attach to mining fatalities between 2015 and 2025 despite the presence of statutory provisions.

That conclusion risks misunderstanding unless placed within the broader architecture of Australian criminal negligence.

Industrial manslaughter is not a regulatory innovation detached from criminal doctrine. It is an application of longstanding principles of criminal negligence adapted to workplace contexts.

To understand why mining prosecutions did not cross that boundary, the underlying doctrine must be examined.

2. The Historical Foundation of Criminal Negligence

Australian criminal negligence derives from common law manslaughter principles.

At common law, negligence becomes criminal only when it constitutes such a gross departure from reasonable care that it merits punishment as a crime rather than a civil wrong.

The High Court in *R v Lavender* (2005) emphasised that criminal negligence requires more than error or inadvertence. It requires a high degree of departure from the standard of care expected of a reasonable person in the circumstances.

This principle is foundational.

Regulatory breach may arise from failure to implement reasonably practicable measures. Criminal negligence requires something qualitatively more serious.

---

3. The "Gross Departure" Standard

The phrase "gross departure" appears frequently in judicial reasoning.

It involves:

- Magnitude of risk
- Probability of harm
- Awareness of danger
- Availability of preventative measures
- Failure to respond

The assessment is contextual.

A minor oversight in a low-risk setting does not approach criminal negligence.

In high-risk industries such as mining, the analysis becomes more complex. The inherent presence of risk does not automatically elevate operational failure to criminal conduct.

Courts must determine whether the conduct demonstrated indifference or recklessness beyond regulatory breach.

---

4. Objective Versus Subjective Elements

Criminal negligence typically incorporates both objective and subjective elements.

Objective:
Would a reasonable person in the accused's position have foreseen the risk?

Subjective:
Did the accused know, or ought they reasonably to have known, of the risk?

In corporate environments, establishing subjective knowledge is particularly complex.

Large organisations distribute decision-making across:

- Boards
- Executives
- Site managers
- Supervisors
- Engineers

Attributing personal criminal negligence requires proof that a specific individual's conduct constituted a gross departure.

In mining prosecutions examined between 2015 and 2025, publicly available records do not demonstrate that individual officers possessed knowledge of imminent lethal probability sufficient to meet this test.

---

5. Corporate Criminal Liability

Industrial manslaughter provisions extend liability to corporate entities.

Corporate criminal negligence requires proof that the corporation's conduct, through its officers or organisational culture, represented a gross departure.

Corporate attribution principles typically require examination of:

- Decision-making structures
- Resource allocation
- Safety culture
- Communication systems

The presence of documented governance frameworks complicates proof of corporate criminal negligence.

Where systems exist, prosecutors must show that they were either illusory or knowingly disregarded.

Mining corporations during the decade examined generally demonstrated structured safety management systems, even where implementation failed.

That distinction weakens arguments of gross indifference.

---

6. Criminal Code and Negligence Thresholds

In jurisdictions operating under Criminal Code principles, negligence is defined as conduct that involves such a great falling short of the standard of care that criminal punishment is warranted.

The threshold is deliberately high.

It reflects a core principle of criminal law: punishment should attach only where conduct demonstrates moral blameworthiness of a significant degree.

Workplace safety statutes do not displace that principle. They incorporate it.

Industrial manslaughter therefore does not lower the criminal negligence threshold. It contextualises it within workplace duty structures.

---

7. Comparative Case Law Outside Mining

Australian criminal negligence cases outside the mining context frequently involve:

- Direct operational control
- Immediate knowledge of lethal conditions
- Explicit warnings ignored
- Continued exposure despite prohibition

Examples across construction, transport and small enterprise contexts demonstrate that where defendants had direct, unambiguous knowledge of life-threatening danger and failed to act, criminal liability followed.

Mining, by contrast, often involves layered risk mitigation systems and technical complexity.

The diffusion of decision-making within mining corporations creates evidentiary friction in establishing singular criminal culpability.

8. The Role of Recklessness

Recklessness differs from negligence.

Recklessness involves conscious awareness of a substantial risk and unjustifiable disregard of that risk.

In mining prosecutions during 2015–2025, Category 1 reckless charges were uncommon in fatal matters.

This suggests that prosecutors assessed available evidence as insufficient to demonstrate subjective awareness of imminent lethal probability.

Absent recklessness, escalation to industrial manslaughter becomes more difficult.

9. Moral Gravity Versus Legal Proof

Fatalities generate moral outrage.

Criminal law, however, operates on proof.

The gravity of consequence does not determine criminal classification.

Courts repeatedly caution against outcome-driven reasoning. The fact that death occurred does not itself prove criminal negligence. The law demands examination of conduct at the time decisions were made, not retrospective judgment after harm materialised.

Mining fatality prosecutions during this decade demonstrate this distinction clearly.

10. Systemic Drift and Organisational Failure

Modern safety scholarship recognises that catastrophic outcomes often arise from gradual system degradation rather than singular conscious decision.

Criminal law traditionally focuses on identifiable acts or omissions.

Bridging systemic organisational drift with individual criminal culpability presents doctrinal difficulty.

Industrial manslaughter provisions attempt to address this by allowing corporate liability.

However, even corporate liability requires proof of gross departure.

Systemic weakness does not automatically equate to criminal negligence.

---

11. The Interaction of Regulatory and Criminal Law

Work health and safety regimes are regulatory in nature.

They aim to:

- Prevent harm
- Encourage compliance
- Promote continuous improvement

Criminal law aims to punish morally blameworthy conduct.

Industrial manslaughter sits at the intersection of these domains.

If criminal law is applied too readily to regulatory breach, doctrinal clarity erodes.

If applied too sparingly, public confidence may suffer.

The mining prosecutions between 2015 and 2025 suggest that courts maintained a clear boundary between regulatory enforcement and criminal sanction.

---

12. The Stability of Doctrine Across Jurisdictions

Western Australia and Queensland differ slightly in legislative wording.

However, the underlying criminal negligence threshold remains consistent.

Across both jurisdictions:

- Gross departure remained the standard.
- Corporate governance complexity affected proof.
- Officer prosecutions were rare.
- Industrial manslaughter convictions did not emerge in mining.

This doctrinal stability reinforces the conclusion that enforcement patterns were not jurisdiction-specific anomalies.

They were reflections of established criminal law principles.

---

13. Implications for Mining Enforcement

Understanding criminal negligence doctrine clarifies why mining prosecutions remained within Category 2 frameworks despite serious outcomes.

It also clarifies what would be required for future industrial manslaughter success:

- Clear documented awareness of lethal probability
- Failure to act despite that awareness
- Evidence of indifference or deliberate disregard
- Absence of meaningful governance structure

Absent those elements, prosecution risk remains substantial.

Conclusion

Industrial manslaughter provisions did not fail between 2015 and 2025.

They operated within the constraints of criminal negligence doctrine.

Mining fatality prosecutions during this decade reveal:

- Serious regulatory breach
- Escalating penalties

- Structured governance systems
- Insufficient evidence of gross criminal departure

The boundary identified in earlier chapters is therefore doctrinal, not political.

It reflects the enduring principles of Australian criminal law.

Chapter References

R v Lavender (2005) 222 CLR 67.

Work Health and Safety Act 2011 (Qld).

Work Health and Safety Act 2020 (WA).

Criminal Code (Qld).

Director of Public Prosecutions (Qld) – Guidelines for Prosecutors.

Office of the Director of Public Prosecutions (WA) – Prosecution Policy.

Safe Work Australia – Model Work Health and Safety Act.

CHAPTER 20

Crossing the Line: A Model Industrial Manslaughter Prosecution in Mining

---

1. Purpose of This Chapter

The preceding chapters demonstrated that industrial manslaughter did not attach to mining fatalities between 2015 and 2025 in Western Australia and Queensland. The evidentiary boundary remained intact.

This chapter asks a different question:

What would it take for that boundary to be crossed?

Rather than speculate abstractly, this chapter constructs a legally grounded model of a mining industrial manslaughter prosecution that would likely succeed under current statutory frameworks.

The purpose is not dramatic effect. It is analytical clarity.

---

2. The Threshold Requirements

For industrial manslaughter to succeed in a mining context, prosecutors would need to establish:

1. A duty existed.
2. The duty was breached.
3. The breach caused death.
4. The conduct constituted criminal negligence.
5. The negligence represented a gross departure from reasonable standards.

The first three elements are common in fatality prosecutions.

The fourth and fifth are the true boundary.

---

3. Model Scenario: Escalating Mobile Plant Risk

Consider an underground mine operating heavy haulage through a curved decline system.

Over a twelve-month period:

• Multiple near miss reports document loss of visibility at a particular intersection.
• A site safety committee recommends installation of proximity detection technology.
• An internal engineering report concludes that without redesign, fatal collision probability is "significant".
• Budget approval for redesign is deferred twice.
• Production quotas increase during the same period.
• A written memorandum from a site engineer states that current configuration "creates unacceptable fatal interaction risk".
• Senior management acknowledges receipt of that memorandum.

Work continues without redesign or interim segregation controls.

A fatal collision occurs at that intersection.

---

4. Evidentiary Escalation

In this model, prosecutors would possess:

• Documented internal fatal risk warnings
• Clear engineering recommendations
• Executive awareness
• Budget deferral decisions
• Continued exposure

This chain establishes:

• Knowledge
• Capacity to act
• Failure to act

• Foreseeable fatal consequence

That matrix is qualitatively different from the prosecutions examined between 2015 and 2025.

---

5. The Officer Exposure Dimension

For officer liability, the prosecution would need to demonstrate:

• The officer had actual knowledge of the fatal risk escalation
• The officer had authority to approve corrective measures
• The officer consciously chose not to implement them
• The decision constituted a gross departure

Minutes of executive meetings, risk registers and email correspondence would be central.

Absent that documentary chain, industrial manslaughter remains fragile.

---

6. Model Scenario: Gas Management Escalation

Consider a coal operation recording repeated methane exceedances above statutory trigger levels.

Over several weeks:

• Trigger action response plans are not fully implemented.
• Ventilation engineering reports recommend withdrawal from a panel.
• Internal communications note ignition probability.
• Production continuity is prioritised.
• Regulator inspection identifies concerns and issues improvement notices.
• Internal audits confirm exceedance patterns.

Operations continue.

An explosion occurs resulting in multiple fatalities.

In this model, the prosecution would rely on:

• Regulator notices

- Internal acknowledgment of lethal probability
- Documented refusal to withdraw
- Causation linking exceedance to ignition

This would present a materially stronger industrial manslaughter case.

---

7. Distinguishing Features from Actual Prosecutions

The key differences between the model and the decade reviewed are:

1. Documented internal fatal probability assessments.
2. Executive-level acknowledgment.
3. Refusal of feasible corrective measures.
4. Regulator warning escalation.
5. Temporal proximity between warning and fatality.

In the prosecuted matters between 2015 and 2025, publicly available records do not reveal this combination.

---

8. The Role of Cost and Disproportionality

Industrial manslaughter would require proof that corrective measures were:

- Available
- Suitable
- Not grossly disproportionate in cost

If cost analysis showed that redesign or technology installation was modest relative to risk, refusal becomes more difficult to justify.

Cost-based deferral in the face of acknowledged lethal probability strengthens criminal negligence arguments.

---

9. Jury Perception and Narrative Coherence

Industrial manslaughter prosecutions are tried in criminal

courts.

The prosecution must present a coherent narrative:

- The risk was known.
- The danger was serious.
- The solution was clear.
- The accused chose not to act.
- Death followed predictably.

Mining fatalities often involve complex chains of technical causation.

Complexity can dilute narrative clarity.

The model scenarios above reduce complexity and increase documentary clarity.

That is why they would likely cross the boundary.

---

10. Governance Collapse as a Precondition

In both model scenarios, governance systems fail not because they are imperfect, but because they are consciously overridden.

The absence of documented override is what insulated mining prosecutions during 2015–2025 from industrial manslaughter escalation.

Where governance operates, even imperfectly, criminal negligence becomes difficult to establish.

Where governance is knowingly overridden, exposure changes fundamentally.

---

11. The Regulatory Response Implication

If future mining prosecutions produce:

- Repeated ignored internal warnings
- Board-level acknowledgment of fatal probability
- Refusal to implement feasible engineering controls

Industrial manslaughter convictions become plausible.

The statutory tools exist.

The question is evidentiary sufficiency.

---

12. The Boundary Clarified

The decade examined demonstrates the boundary.

The model demonstrates the crossing.

The difference lies in:

- Documentation
- Knowledge
- Refusal
- Escalation

Without those elements, industrial manslaughter remains legally remote.

With them, it becomes prosecutorially viable.

Conclusion

Industrial manslaughter in mining is not unattainable.

It is evidentiary.

Between 2015 and 2025, mining fatality prosecutions did not present the documentary chain necessary to establish gross criminal departure.

Future cases may differ.

The statutory framework is in place.

The boundary is not symbolic.

It is structural.

Crossing it requires proof of conscious disregard, not operational failure alone.

Chapter References

Work Health and Safety Act 2011 (Qld).

Work Health and Safety Act 2020 (WA).
R v Lavender (2005) 222 CLR 67.
Safe Work Australia – Model Work Health and Safety Act.
Director of Public Prosecutions (Qld) – Prosecution Guidelines.
Office of the Director of Public Prosecutions (WA) – Prosecution Policy.

EVIDENTIARY BOUNDARIES AND LIMITATIONS

This manuscript analyses fatal mining prosecutions within defined evidentiary boundaries. It relies exclusively on publicly available judgments, sentencing remarks, regulator releases and legislative instruments.

Several limitations should be acknowledged.

First, prosecution summaries and sentencing remarks do not capture the entirety of investigative material. Prosecutorial briefs often contain detailed internal communications, witness interviews and expert reports not reproduced in full within published judgments. Accordingly, this analysis is confined to evidence placed before the court and publicly recorded.

Second, the absence of industrial manslaughter convictions in mining during 2015–2025 does not equate to absence of industrial manslaughter conduct. It reflects only that, in prosecuted matters during this period, evidentiary thresholds were not met or charges were not pursued at that level.

Third, legislative reform is ongoing. Amendments introduced late in the decade may influence future prosecution patterns beyond the scope of this analysis.

Fourth, mining operations vary significantly in scale, commodity and governance structure. While systemic patterns are observable, they do not eliminate operational diversity.

Finally, legal interpretation evolves. Appellate clarification of criminal negligence standards in other industries may influence future mining prosecutions.

The findings within this manuscript therefore represent a structured analysis of a defined historical period. They establish a baseline. They do not predict inevitability.

The legal threshold remains constant. Evidence determines whether it is crossed.

APPENDIX A

Legislative Architecture Summary (Mining Fatality Framework 2015–2025)

This appendix summarises the statutory architecture referenced throughout this manuscript. It is not exhaustive legislative reproduction. It identifies the core provisions underpinning mining fatality prosecutions during the decade examined.

Western Australia

Work Health and Safety Act 2020 (WA)

Primary Duty of Care
Reckless Conduct Offence
Industrial Manslaughter Offence
Officer Due Diligence Obligations

Work Health and Safety (Mines) Regulations 2022 (WA)

Ground control obligations
Ventilation and atmospheric monitoring
Plant and equipment safety
Traffic management
Emergency response

Queensland

Work Health and Safety Act 2011 (Qld)

Primary duty provisions
Category 1 Reckless Conduct

Industrial Manslaughter (introduced 2017 amendments)
Officer Due Diligence

Coal Mining Safety and Health Act 1999 (Qld)
Mining and Quarrying Safety and Health Act 1999 (Qld)

Site senior executive obligations
Safety and health management systems
Risk assessment and control

New South Wales

Work Health and Safety Act 2011 (NSW)

Primary duty
Category 1 Reckless Conduct
Industrial Manslaughter (introduced 2020 amendments)
Officer Due Diligence

Work Health and Safety (Mines and Petroleum Sites) Act 2013 (NSW)

Principal hazard management
Safety management systems
Notification and reporting obligations

Elements of Primary Duty Prosecutions

To establish primary duty breach in fatal mining matters, prosecutors must prove:

Existence of duty
Failure to ensure health and safety so far as reasonably practicable
Exposure to risk
Causation where death results

Elements of Category 1 Reckless Conduct

Exposure to risk of death or serious injury
Recklessness as to that risk

Recklessness requires awareness of risk and conscious disregard.

Elements of Industrial Manslaughter

Existence of duty
Conduct causing death
Criminal negligence or recklessness of high order

The threshold is materially higher than breach.

Officer Due Diligence

Officers must:

Acquire knowledge of WHS matters
Understand operational hazards
Ensure appropriate resources
Ensure reporting processes
Verify implementation

Failure to exercise due diligence may result in personal liability.

APPENDIX B

Comparative Penalty and Prosecution Matrix (2015–2025)

This matrix summarises structural patterns observed across mining fatality prosecutions during the decade examined.

Hazard Domains Prosecuted
Mobile plant interaction
Ground and strata instability
Mechanical isolation
Explosion and gas
Fatigue-related exposure

Typical Charge Category
Primary duty breach
Occasional reckless conduct
No industrial manslaughter convictions in mining during period examined

Officer Prosecution Frequency
Limited
Dependent on documented awareness

Sentencing Patterns
Substantial corporate fines
Calibration to seriousness and mitigation
No custodial sentences in mining industrial manslaughter during period examined

Escalation Determinant
Documentation of knowledge
Causation clarity
Implementation versus abandonment

APPENDIX C

Structured Analytical Model for Mining Fatality Exposure

This model consolidates the framework developed in Chapter 15.

Step 1: Identify documented hazard systems
Step 2: Assess implementation integrity
Step 3: Map escalation pathways
Step 4: Analyse documentary knowledge trail
Step 5: Map officer awareness
Step 6: Evaluate resource allocation decisions
Step 7: Assess causation clarity
Step 8: Apply statutory threshold

This model reflects evidentiary patterns observed between 2015 and 2025 and may assist in future exposure assessment.

METHODOLOGY AND SOURCE INTEGRITY STATEMENT

This manuscript is confined to publicly available material between 2015 and 2025. Sources relied upon include:

Court sentencing remarks
Published judgments
Regulator prosecution summaries
Legislative instruments
Parliamentary amendment records
Official guidance materials
Publicly available technical reports

No reliance has been placed on speculative commentary or unpublished material.

Where judicial reasoning is referenced, the analysis is grounded in the language of the court rather than secondary interpretation.

Case selection was limited to fatal mining matters prosecuted within Australian jurisdictions during the period examined. Non-mining matters are referenced only for comparative threshold analysis.

Legislative analysis reflects statutory provisions in force at the time of prosecution. Where amendments occurred during the period examined, the applicable version at time of offence has been referenced.

The analytical framework developed in Chapters 15 and 16 is derived from recurring patterns observable in documented prosecutions. It is descriptive rather than predictive and does not represent regulatory guidance.

This manuscript does not seek to re-litigate factual findings. It examines how those findings interacted with statutory architecture.

All references are capable of independent verification.

MASTER REFERENCE LIST

Department of Mines, Industry Regulation and Safety (DMIRS) (2015–2025) *Prosecution Media Releases and Annual Reports*. Government of Western Australia.

Director of Public Prosecutions (Queensland) (current version) *Guidelines for Prosecutors*. Office of the Director of Public Prosecutions, Queensland.

Office of the Director of Public Prosecutions (Western Australia) (current version) *Prosecution Policy and Guidelines*. Government of Western Australia.

Parliament of Queensland (2017) *Explanatory Notes: Work Health and Safety and Other Legislation Amendment Bill 2017 (Qld).*

Parliament of Western Australia (2019) *Work Health and Safety Bill 2019 – Second Reading Speech.*

Resources Safety and Health Queensland (RSHQ) (2015–2025) *Prosecution Summaries, Safety Alerts and Annual Performance Reports*. Queensland Government.

R v Lavender (2005) 222 CLR 67.

Safe Work Australia (2011) *Model Work Health and Safety Act*. Canberra: Safe Work Australia.

Safe Work Australia (various years) *Work-Related Traumatic Injury Fatalities Reports*. Canberra: Safe Work Australia.

Work Health and Safety Act 2011 (Qld).

Work Health and Safety Act 2020 (WA).

Criminal Code Act 1899 (Qld).

Mines Safety and Inspection Act 1994 (WA) (historical).

Mining and Quarrying Safety and Health Act 1999 (Qld) (historical).

Resources Safety and Health Act 2020 (Qld).

Queensland Coal Mining Safety and Health Regulation (historical versions applicable during period examined).

REFERENCE-TO-CHAPTER MAPPING TABLE

Legislative Framework Mapping

Reference	Chapters Used	Purpose
Work Health and Safety Act 2011 (Qld)	8–20	Officer duty, IM provisions, Category offences
Work Health and Safety Act 2020 (WA)	8–20	WA IM framework and officer liability
Resources Safety and Health Act 2020 (Qld)	3–7, 12	Mining-specific enforcement context
Mining and Quarrying Safety and Health Act 1999 (Qld)	3–6	Historical mining enforcement context
Mines Safety and Inspection Act 1994 (WA)	3–6	Pre-harmonised WA framework
Criminal Code Act 1899 (Qld)	17–19	Criminal negligence doctrine

Case Law Mapping

Case	Chapters Used	Purpose
R v Lavender (2005) 222 CLR 67	17, 19	High Court articulation of criminal negligence threshold

Prosecutorial Policy Mapping

Source	Chapters Used	Purpose
DPP (Qld) Guidelines for Prosecutors	18–20	Reasonable prospect test and charge discretion
DPP (WA) Prosecution Policy	18–20	Charging threshold analysis

Regulator Enforcement Mapping

Source	Chapters Used	Purpose
DMIRS Prosecution Media Releases (2015–2025)	3–7, 12, 16	WA enforcement patterns
RSHQ Prosecution Summaries (2015–2025)	3–7, 12, 16	QLD enforcement patterns
RSHQ Safety Alerts	4–6	Hazard domain analysis
Safe Work Australia Fatality Reports	3, 12, 16	Statistical fatality context

Parliamentary Intent Mapping

Source	Chapters Used	Purpose

Qld Explanatory Notes (2017 IM reforms)	9, 17	Legislative intent
WA Second Reading Speech (2019 WHS Bill)	9, 17	IM rationale

Made in United States
North Haven, CT
04 November 2026

21763947R00085